SKETC OF SPAIN
ONE MAN'S GUIDE TO SPAIN AND PORTUGAL

Duncan Gough

Duncan Gough

Buen viaje!

"I travel not to go anywhere, but to go."

Robert Louis Stevenson

For my mother and *mis amigos* who share my love of travel, and of the back roads of any country

A sound track to this book is the Miles Davis album - 'Sketches of Spain'

First published by Matador 2016

Revised Second Edition 2017

By Hombre Publishing
Bronheulog, Ceredigion. SY23 3BE, Wales.
Tel: 01970 625580
Web: www.duncan-spanish-travel.com
Twitter: @duncangough
ISBN 978-0-9957454-1-4
British Library Cataloguing in Publication Data.
A catalogue record for this book is available from the British Library.
Typeset in Segue UI 12pt by Hombre

Printed by Zenith Media
centre for printing excellence

HOMBRE

Contents

Introduction

This book represents the fruits of over 30 years of Spanish trips. It is a personal view and there are as many ways to enjoy Spain as there are *tapas*. I hope there will be things here that the reader is not aware of and suggestions that will enhance your own Spanish adventure. I have deliberately not gone into great detail about all the sights and points of interest in the cities, this information is comprehensively available via the internet.

Although written from mainly motorbike journeys it is applicable to other forms of transport. Just use your common sense.

Travelling in Spain is a wonderful experience, a new landscape to enjoy, great food and wine. An exceptionally friendly and accepting people and culture. Children are welcomed nearly everywhere and very rarely excluded from adult life.

I meet a lot of people who treat a holiday in Spain like a trip to Blackpool: We must get past Madrid tonight so we can make 'Touristville' as soon as possible. Or like an American 'doing' Europe; Madrid – tick, Granada – tick, Paris... I've had Americans requesting a guided tour of Wales in a day!

Start your holiday the minute you are on Spanish soil, there are marvellous places and sights to see, if you just take a little more time. So what if you have two days less in your villa. On the way you will have eased into the real Spain, travelled safer, and begun an adventure you will never forget.

I make no apologies for sticking bits of Spanish throughout this book, every little helps and I am sure you can work them out.

Spain is like its food, not to be lashed with salt and vinegar and thrown down. Savour each different dish, sip a cold *cerveza* or taste the sun in a glass of *rioja* as you watch and greet the passing *gente*.

I think of Spain as a dining table that has had the tablecloth dropped over all the crockery and cutlery. Once you climb onto the table there are many ranges of hills and mountains and quiet river valleys to find. Each *pueblo* or *ciudad* alike but also unique. Always a Plaza Mayor, a central square virtually always pedestrian to a large extent; a mark of the 'community' of the Spanish ethos, here the community meets and embraces itself.

Many times when I have stopped to check my map I have had pedestrians or car drivers stop and ask me *"Que Pasa?"* Or ask if I was lost and needed help. Spain is a very, very friendly place. If you strike up any kind of communication in a bar you may find your coffee paid for, if there is a wedding or a fiesta where you happen to be you may be included by default in the event. It never hurts to make a little effort; - *"Este pueblo es muy bonito"*. "This village is very pretty."

The aim of this book is to provide practical advice for travelling, as well as a resource for planning your 'adventure'. Read right through and pick the places you like the sound of, look at the map in relation to your journey and see which places can be fitted into your itinerary.

The 'Really Useful Stuff', is a section dedicated to legal requirements when driving/riding in Spain and Portugal and safety tips, as well as something of the way I go about my Iberian adventures. For me adventure is about a bit of stretching, and that stretching is what counts, whether it be walking where you have never been in your own city or climbing Everest. Wherever your edge is, push it a bit. In Spain make the most of every day. Be flexible, go back-roads first and 'Rough Guide/Google' second, get the history and details when you've finally decided where you are going to end up.

The enemy of adventure is predestined package adherence to a 'holiday plan'.

I find maps, preferably 1:350,000 more use than a SatNav. You can see the wider picture better and spot features that may be worth investigation.

I rarely go to the *costas*. I want to see Spain, not 'touristville' so I tend to stay 80 miles or so inland.

There are some small extracts from my previous book 'Back Roads of Spain'.

A NOTE ON ROAD NUMBERING. Please double check road numbers with a current map as it is not uncommon for the numbers to be changed between one year and the next, or be re-built into an *autopista de peaje* - toll motorway, *autopista* or *autovia* - dual carriageway, instead of the good old back road it was!

FRANCE

amplona   Jaca

o

Sos del Rey Católico

Barcelona

RIO EBRO

ia

Zaragoza

Alcorisa

Cuenca

Valencia

Cañón Rio Júcar

Albacete

Alicante

Yecla

ESPAÑA

A Long Way Round

Hang a Right

A Spanish Backbone

Other

ernas

eria

<u>Prologue</u>

A typical back road happenstance

Coming lunchtime and just what I am looking for:- water running from a plastic pipe but with a drinking cup left beside the *fuente de beber* close to a crude table and bench. No need for signs attesting to the water quality, the locals - *gente local,* obviously use this spring. I unpack my bread, Mahou, sausage and cheese *(pan, cerveza, chorizo y manchego)* and catch a large draft of clear, cold spring water.

What a feast. A warbler sings a few phrases in the brush, but gives up. It is siesta time... I stretch out on the table and close my eyes.

A symphony is playing. The silky, satin rustle of the *hojas de chopo* - poplar leaves that crowd over the little river across the road, their subtle playing fades and rises as a small breeze conducts. The water falling from the pipe

is a tympani and the string section is headed up by the cicadas that rasp and fiddle in the afternoon heat. The breeze-conductor sometimes holds up his baton and they all stop instantly for a few breaths, and perhaps the hardy little leaves of the oak trees get a chance to perform or from the river bottom comes a burst of liquid bird song.

This is the true wealth of back road travel. Hot maybe dusty miles have been travelled, maybe not all easy ones. But when you stop in an oasis like this and shed the movement, place yourself entirely HERE, all the rest comes into focus, the whole tapestry gains dimension. These moments are the true jewels in the 'going', a nowhere place, unknown to the internet, on no map but those of the local villagers who pass and use it. And for a brief time, ALL MINE!

Another time I drifted out to the little *pueblo* of Huérmeces for lunch. A *café solo*, then a piece of *tortilla* and a *caña*. The couple who run the Bar Los Faroles now know my occasional face and *la señora* handed me a new brochure for the valley/*cañón* of the Rio Urbel. So I went to explore and look for a spot for my siesta. I turned off on the track/road to San Pantaleón del Páramo and then up a dirt track into the beginnings of a tight little *cañón*. I love these moments in Spain. I put down the side stand and there is no traffic sound, the cicadas have stilled but will soon restart their insistent rumour-ance. The midday sun is baking the land and smells are intensified. The wild herbs; thymes and rosemaries are having their oils burnt off into the hot air for my benefit, orchids gleam and the dust I disturbed on arrival settles leaving only a hot stony tang. I spread my riding jacket, take a

long drink of the still cool water from the fountain in Huérmeces and settle back to meditate for my 20 minute siesta; sinking myself into the sounds and scents of a Spanish summer's afternoon. Suddenly my peace is broken by a horrific barking and growling. 'Hound of the Baskervilles' stuff! After an initial wild surge of adrenalin I recognise it as a *corzo* - roe deer buck, and relax. It had nearly walked right over me, it went off 'humphing' annoyance!

Bilbao to Burgos

As I said in the Introduction, I believe in easing one's way into the rich waters of Spain and MY way out from the ferry terminal will do that. Of course, if you are committed to being in Madrid/Malaga by nightfall, take the motorways that you will be directed to. Bye...

My preference is to only go a hundred-odd miles on day one and stay in the wonderful city of Burgos, for me the gateway to Spain. If you are going to the Picos and Asturias/Galicia or the Pyrenees it is perhaps a detour, though one that might just be worth making to see the *meseta* and the plains of Don Quixote's land! My Burgos routes will give you a tantalising first look at the wonders of Spain's back roads.

The ferry does not actually dock in Bilbao, but has moved westward, and now docks nearly 20 km out at Zierbena.

Off the ferry on the second roundabout take the first right to Zierbena, this is the original little fishing village and is *España inmediatamente*. You might like to stop by the little roundabout at the head of the harbour and go get a coffee and a croissant. Or head onward...

There is a traffic light for the road up through the town but do keep an eye out for joining traffic which is not controlled. There are two ways to get up to the San Roque Auzoa road, but basically head inland and upward. You

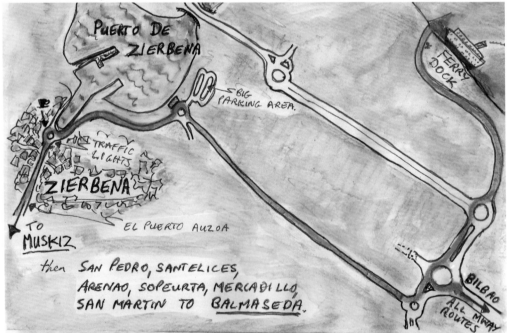

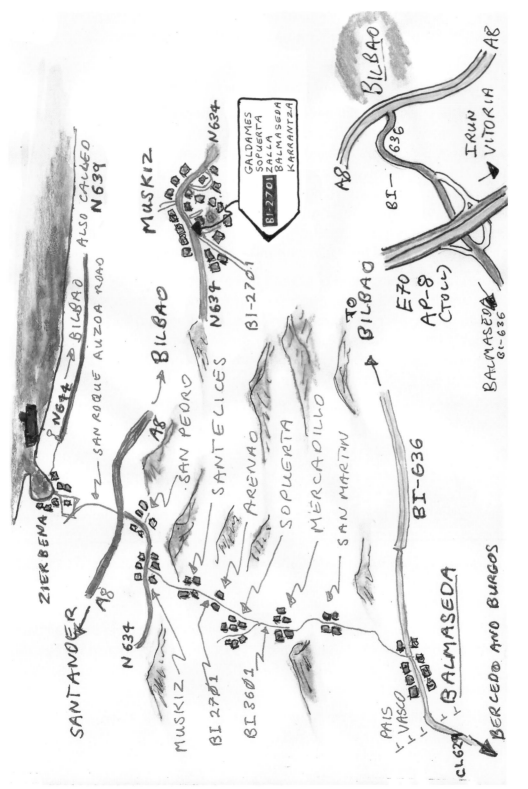

are heading for San Pedro and then Muskiz so you could SatNav it for the shortest route to Muskiz, might be interesting... Pass under the A-8.

In Muskiz you want to pick up the BI-2701 road through Santelices and Arenao for Sopuerta and ultimately Balmaseda.

This route is on Michelin white roads but don't be put off, they are rural but are nearly all well surfaced, (unless there are works - *obras*), with great views as you come up through the Cantabrian mountain range. Take your time, smell the eucalyptus and pines, stop and listen to the sounds of rural Spain. Balmaseda is a bustling little town on both sides of the river and you might like to stop there for refreshment and a wander. A bit further on at Bercedo there is a petrol station with, as is often the case, a great bar and shop, they do a brill *bocadillo* with *tortilla* filling, and it is easy to park up.

There is an alternative way of getting there via the motorway passing Bilbao (for Pamplona and Vitoria) and picking up the slip road for Balmaseda, BL-636 off the A-8. There is a new AP-8 - E-70 being built (Toll) which will probably get signposted Pamplona/Vitoria/Burgos/Madrid. If you end up on it you should be able to get off onto the BI-636 though the slip road might take you a bit back towards Bilbao.

I have different routes from shortly after Bercedo depending on time and weather.

The longer route will take you via the spectacular castle at Poza de la Sal. The other is a faster way towards Burgos but also has some great roads and views. Going to Poza just after Bercedo you want to get onto the N-629. In fact you could have come all the way from Laredo halfway between Bilbao and Santander on it if you didn't fancy threading up from Muskiz.

You will pass Medina de Pomar and then arrive at Trespaderne. If camping, you might like to check out the reasonable campsite for a possible last night before the return run to the outbound ferry.

Oña is another nice place for a coffee or even perhaps a *caña* or small beer. Continue down the N-232 till you get to Cornudilla, keep a sharp eye out for the signs for Poza de la Sal (there is an earlier road through Salas de Bureba), BU-502.

When you get to Poza continue up through the little town and you will pass through a very narrow opening under a huge cliff on top of which is the Rojas Castle (9th to 15th century). Down to the right are Roman salt pans. The road is now a series of very steep hairpin bends so I hope your

low speed control is good. Keep checking the road above for anything coming down. It straightens up a bit as you get round to the back of the spine of rock and there is a turning to the left onto a dirt road (not too bad at all, but if you don't like it park up and walk), that takes you to the foot of the castle. ENJOY! The views from the top are fantastic. You might like to imagine being a Moor and trying to assault this. Look for the defensive traps built into the castle design. Probably don't go up if you suffer from vertigo...

This is a land for eagles and vultures. As you stand on the top of the castle you will get an eagle's eye view of the country and probably observe high Griffon Vultures or maybe a Booted Eagle.

You can then continue on up the valley and top out on a high plain with a big wind farm. The road is (last time I was on it), rather bumpy so I ride in the middle which is slightly better (unless of course another vehicle is coming). Hit the CL-629 and join the shorter route and truck on down toward Burgos. OR, if you still have time in hand (remember the Spanish generally don't eat till at the earliest 8pm), then you could cross-over the CL-629 and head for the neat little village of Masa, then you can cross the N-623 from Santander and continue on real back roads to the N-627. Don't get too carried away with the empty road and curves, the locals won't expect to meet anyone either.

On the quick route just after Bercedo you turn off onto the CL-629

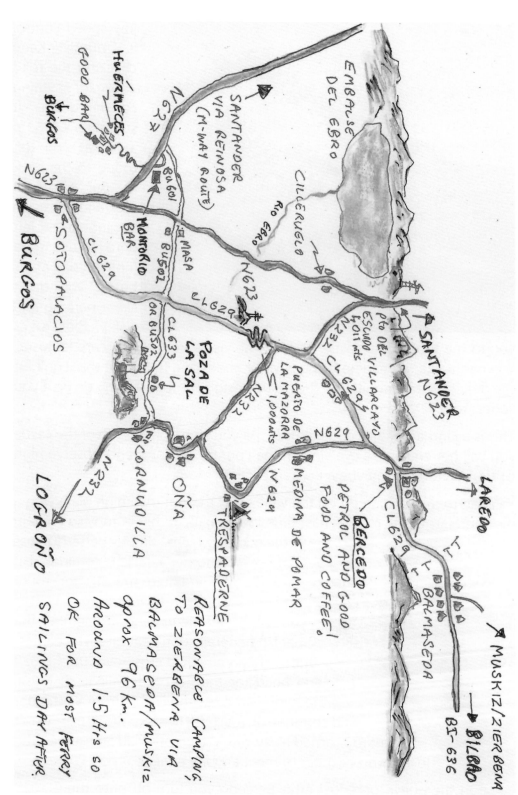

for Villarcayo just after which you join the N-232 for a short stretch to Valdenoceda where you again pick up the CL-629 and go up a pretty good switchback pass to Puerto de Mazorra (1,000 mts). It was even better years ago before they sanitised it! As you get over the top of the pass you can take a right up a short track to the Mirador underneath the TV and mobile aerial tower. Stop a moment and take in the breadth and size of the land, the towering Cantabrian mountains behind you, the distance and the breadth of the great Spanish sky.

Puerto de Mazorra - Cantabrian cloud

A lot of people think Spain is always hot, in fact it has very variable weather and temperatures. One can sit in a bar in Granada in 45 degrees and gaze up at the southernmost permanent snow in Europe on the top of the Sierra Nevada! You can get torrential rain and thunderstorms with hail in the middle of June and snow banks a 100 miles from Santander.

If you have now reached the N-627 you might like a break for some *tapas*, now you are nearly at Burgos. Turning left toward Burgos you will use the central slip lane when joining the main carriageway. Very soon you will have signs to Montorio going left. Here there is quite a big restaurant and bar which is normally always open as it seems a lot of truckers and road crews use it (very good sign of quality). I'm pretty sure it was here that I once had *callos* that was actually very nice. *Callos* is cooked intestine and here it was in a nice sauce of garlic and tomatoes, elsewhere I have had it and it was a rather grim, grey boiled mess.

A nice alternative is the much smaller bar in Huérmeces, reached by turning next right off the N-627 onto BU-622. It also gives you one of those reasons for trying the back roads, a lovely hidden river valley (Rio Urbel) through which the road winds between quite high rocky cliffs. I have seen Golden Eagles here, and there are Neolithic caves up in those cliffs.

The valley opens out. At the right time of the year you may be treated to a

blush of cerise poppies across the viridian field of barley, stretching toward the beckoning *pueblo*.

As you enter the village take a left off the main road where, high on the wall there is a sign for the 'Bar Los Faroles', follow round the street. A little further on a 'San Miguel' sign sticks out from the wall, here is the bar and restaurant. Check out the oven and the stuffed boar's head. One year when the owner told me about the caves, I went back to look for them. I stopped where I thought they were and shortly he drove up; he had come to make sure I had found them.

Hostal Acuarela in Burgos is 30 km away, half an hour. By the way hostals in Spain are NOT hostels with dormitories but are small family run hotels and are generally very good value and cheaper than hotels.

Huérmeces

Santander to Burgos

Santander is quite unusual in a way because the ferry ties up pretty much on the town front, next to a park across which there are shopping areas and the central town. There is the conventional dockside to the east, and it is through this that you are now directed out to the beginnings of the motorways. In the good old days everyone spewed out onto the roundabout by the park and the Guardia Civil periodically held up the local traffic to send all the *extranjeros* off inland. Now, going straight out through the docks you pass through a lot of warehouses so be careful of lorries and don't speed, I have seen Guardia lurking along here.

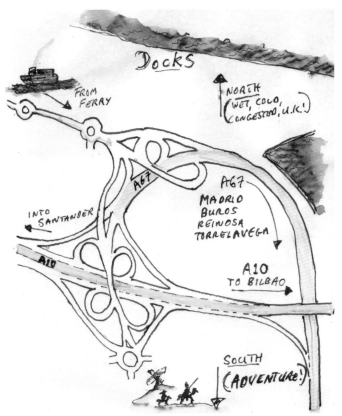

Eventually after going over a bridge across a bit of dock you come to the main roundabout for exiting Santander. East for Bilbao and the Pyrenees runs the S-10. West for pretty much all the rest is the A-67, this is the big motorway variously signed Madrid, Torrelavega, Burgos and Oviedo. My preferred route to Burgos is to pick up the N-623 which, when I started coming to Spain, was the main route south. Now they try and send you on the motorway past Torrelavega and Reinosa toward Madrid and 'by the by' Burgos.

You start by following Burgos signs, but as soon as I am on the A-67 passing underneath the S-10 motorway and across some open land I keep my eyes peeled for the N-623 slip road which comes up next. The first slip road will say Santander Centro, then there is an 'on' slip road and then the one you want; N-623 for Vargas and Muriedas.

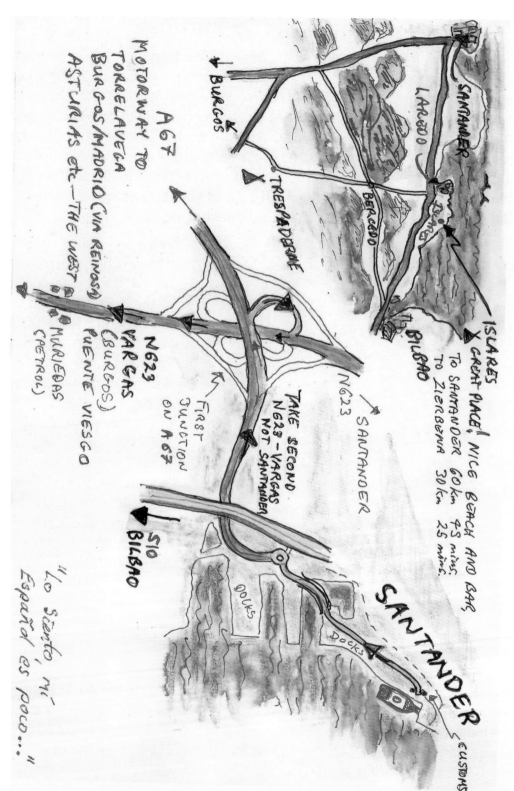

A67

MOTORWAY TO
TORRELAVEGA
BURGOS/MADRID (VIA REINOSA)
ASTURIAS etc — THE WEST

↓ BURGOS

X TRESPADERNE

N623
VARGAS
(BURGOS)
PUENTE VIESGO

← FIRST
JUNCTION
ON A67

↓ MURIEDAS
(PETROL)

TAKE SECOND
N623 - VARGAS
NOT SANTANDER

N623

SANTANDER →

STO
BILBAO

LAREDO

SANTANDER

BERCEDO

BILBAO

ISLARES
X GREAT PLACE!! NICE BEACH AND BARS
TO SANTANDER 60 km, 45 mins.
TO ZIERBEÑA 30 km, 25 mins.

← CUSTOMS

DOCKS

Docks

SANTANDER

"Lo siento, mi
Español es poco..."

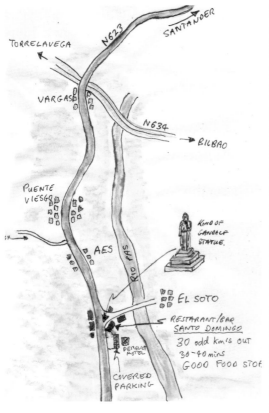

Muriedas has a petrol station if you need it. Mostly the next few kilometres is fairly urban as you pass through the outskirts of Santander. Roundabouts and junctions are all good because your concentration is up and you are getting the feel for Spanish roads and traffic. This route, within the hour brings you to the Bar and Restaurant Santo Domingo. It was a very 'local', very 'Spanish' place, and maybe still is. Though it has now moved into brand new premises where the old motel was. But it still has a covered parking area, which is nice if it happens to be 'moist' this side of the Cantabrian Mountains. For me this a good time to stop, if only for a *"café solo, por favor"* and to really feel myself '*en España*'.

Feeling refreshed I saddle up and start the 30-odd kilometres to the top of the Cantabrians at Puerto del Escudo, 1011 mts (3,300'). Higher than Snowdon!

The N-623 is a lovely road to ride; the steep hairpin bends of the climb up the Cantabrians, the little villages having the steeper roofs and half-timbered upper floors typical of the lands of the Costa Verde. Over the top and Spain spreads out its distance before you, and if you have been in cloud or rain it nearly always clears at the Puerto. The inland sea of the Embalse de Ebro and the distant plains of La Mancha beckon the *caballero*. A high-blasted heathland leads to the drop down into the steep walled Ebro valley. Green with whispering poplars and the rushing river. Coming down the switchbacks into the Ebro *cañón* always brings back memories of stopping to look at the view with my Dad, on the way to work near Valencia. The colours and grandeur of the Spanish scenery are always enhanced for me by memories of his artistic view. Architecture changing again, though we are still in lands that can get a lot of snow in winter. The road has the tall striped snow poles along its higher more windswept parts. Finally you come out of the winding *desfiladeros* and on to the plain leading to Burgos.

It depends on the time of day, the weather, and your inclination...

If I have the time, I always take the route that includes Poza de la Sal, I never tire of the incredible feeling of history, from the Roman onward.

There are many good hotels in Burgos but I always stay in one of two friendly hostals. As mentioned earlier, a hostal is just a small, often family run hotel and they are good value. Hostal Acuarela is close to the Plaza de España near the centre of the city. It's very modern and has a lift to the underground parking area which is not huge, you might like to book a spot. Every room has a laptop connected to the Internet and there is a self-

service area for breakfast that is open the rest of the time for making yourself a cup of coffee or whatever. Hostal Acanto is out on the N-1 Vitoria road in Gamonal. It has underground parking, is clean and modern but a bit quieter and cheaper than Acuarela. From just outside Acanto you can catch the number 1 Gamonal bus right to the El Cid statue in the city centre for a euro or so, it runs

This little boy parked his *moto* next to mine, but was a bit shy about the photo.

till midnight normally and probably 2am on fiestas. I admit both these hostals are owned by friends of mine, a very friendly family that I have known for years, starting with the time they helped me by ringing round to find me the specific back tyre I needed after squaring it off coming down through France.

Burgos Cathedral, gilded with evening light.

There is also camping at Fuentes Blancas, this is a very reasonable municipal campsite, with its own restaurant etc. But you will probably want to go into town. Unfortunately the last bus to town is 7.30pm and the last back is 7.15pm! Hmm... Wonder if the local taxi companies have anything to do with it. But if there is more than one of you a taxi back at the end of the night is not going to be expensive.

Once settled you will of course go out for a *paseo*. The *paseo* is a Spanish tradition, a stroll around your town or village centre.

Passing through the Plaza Mayor and going left, or going along the *espolón* by the river and through the Arco de Santa Maria brings you to the Cathedral. Climb up the many steps to the castle for a fantastic view over the city.

Arco de Santa María and a view from the castle.

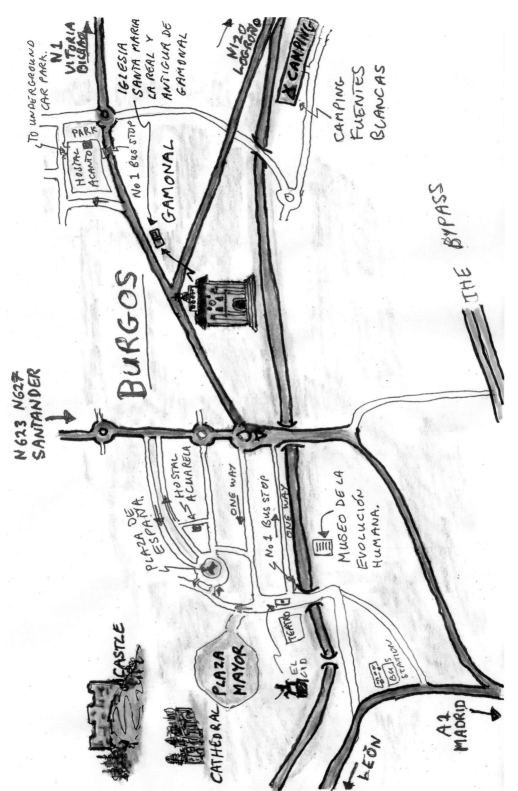

Burgos

What a great day that was, getting here, and then the evening *paseo*...

If you travel this wonderful country you will probably find one village or city where you just feel at home, always welcome and never tired of it. For me that is Burgos. You may find that Salamanca, Cuenca or Barcelona ticks your boxes. It is worth the time to find the one that does.

I always carry a sketchbook and I just love sitting under the interlocking branches of the plane trees in Burgos, with a cup of coffee or a glass of *rioja* and scribbling something for my own memories. I have a conceit about Burgos being my city: I have a supposed family tree that goes back to Edward the First King of England (I keep quiet about that in Wales and Scotland), who married Eleanor of Castilla in Burgos. She was the love of his life, nursed him through a poisoned dagger attack when he was on crusade in the Holy Land. On her tragic death in the north he erected beautiful stone crosses wherever her coffin rested on its way to London: Lincoln, Grantham, Stamford, Geddington, Northampton, Stony Stratford, Woburn, Dunstable, St. Albans, Waltham, Cheapside, and Charing.

This is my city. Often I book my first night in Spain in the Hostal Acanto. Coming out of town on the Calle Vitoria you will see the Iglesia Santa Maria on your right. This is a lovely church and is on the Camino de Santiago

Espolón de Burgos

- the Pilgrims' Way to Santiago de Compostela (St James of the Field of Stars). You can make a left turn just after it and go round the block to where the underground car park entrance is, though you need to get the key - *llave* from reception when you book in. On a bike you can also go straight on round the roundabout and carefully mount the pavement where the car park comes out on the corner of the block. If you are careful and respectful, nobody will mind you going along the pavement and parking up in front of the hostal reception to book in and unload. After a shower I wander out to the bus stop and catch the Gamonal bus into the city centre. Just ask for *"centro"* and you'll get it. You end up close to the statue of El Cid in front of the Teatro Principal from which the main *paseo* or *espolón* stretches along by the river.

There are many things to see in Burgos, as you'd expect for a city of this size and antiquity.

It's one of those things I love about Spain, the whole sense of community and a society that is very easy with itself for the most part, particularly I guess in the more provincial areas. Even outside of fiesta time the Plaza Mayor in the evenings is filled with families meeting and greeting friends and relations. A young teenage boy walks across the square with his arm round his shorter father's shoulders, pats him on the back before he goes to chat with some of his mates. On Sunday's *paseo* you can still see little boys in their traditional sailor suits and little girls be-ribboned and be-bowed.

Though I have seen the square used more seriously. In 2000 I wrote:

'In the Plaza Mayor a silent demonstration: a banner with two white hands. People gather in a big half circle facing the Town Hall with its huge flags drifting in the slight breeze. Quiet, totally silent this area, further out across the plaza still children run, and chase the pigeons screaming, laughing.

Near they are quietly hushed. An old man has two pretty little girls in the same green dresses with bows in their hair, one within the circle of each arm. Each holds a piece of cardboard cut from a box with the letters 'ETANO' on it. It takes a minute to realise it says "E.T.A. NO". He holds them in front of him, a hand cradled round each brown face as they silently stand facing. There are three and then more TV cameras and newspaper photographers who film the silent standing crowd that grows as passers-by who come to see what is happening and join. Two policeman watch from the outer edges of the crowd. I can sense that though the crowd is silent it could be aroused, that there is a deep anger against ETA.'

Throughout Spain the Plaza Mayor belongs to *toda la gente* - all the people.

My little free map of the city, picked up from the hostal, lists 55 buildings of historical interest. I dare say a read through the 'Rough Guide' or similar will give you plenty of further ideas depending on the sort of things that interest you.

When I first started coming regularly to Burgos, often only for a few days, I would enjoy the city in the evenings and during the days explore the surrounding area. I quickly found, and came to love the nearby Sierra de la Demanda, but there are also some great places to the north, back up towards the Cantabrians. Frias and Briviesca in particular. Frias which is not far from Trespaderne also has a campsite and the town is more interesting.

In the last 17 years of my annual visits to Burgos there have been a number of changes. One year, the cathedral covered in scaffolding as it was cleaned, which made a great difference to the beauty of the stonework, shining out after the years of grey grime that had clothed it. The Plaza Mayor was completely resurfaced, after the underground car park underneath had been renovated and given new entrances, exits and lifts. This is a clever, common phenomenon in Spain where every town has a Plaza Mayor - keep it pedestrian and stick a multi-storey car park underneath. The by-passing of the city has got bigger and further out. More recently there has been a well designed redevelopment of a section of the N-120 that ran on the south bank of the Rio Arlanzón. Pedestrian park area and amenities have been created which front new buildings, including the fascinating Museo de la Evolución Humana - Museum of Human Evolution. Atapuerca just to the north of Burgos is of international importance in the story of hominids in Europe and the link with the museum is very strong. Visiting it is a unique experience that I would thoroughly recommend, the huge, airy open space

on three mezzanine floors is impressive enough but the way in which all the exhibits partake of the space makes it unusual and continually interesting.

If you come to Burgos in the last week of June you can catch the Fiestas de San Pedro y San Pablo, locally known as *Sampedros*. There are absolutely massive fireworks displays, parades and bands, concerts, (the Taverners were playing in 2015), and loads of kiosks serving a tapa and a wine or beer for €2.20. The last night ended, at least the concert across from Hostal Acuarela, at 4am! Apart from the scheduled events there are many spontaneous things happening.

For some tapas find Pecaditos just off the Plaza Mayor, here everything is one euro, write your name on the top of the list of tapas and drinks, choose what you want, and wait to have your name shouted out to collect and pay - fantastic value. I was enjoying my food when one of the bands that had

been active in the parades started doing some impromptu playing for a little girl to dance to. Everybody is out enjoying themselves till all hours, very few drunks and I have never seen a fight or argument.

There are so many special places to find for yourself. So I am not naming them all, cos' that takes away from your discoveries; this is not a McDoncBurger menu of a book. Okay! For tapas, El Polvorilla (Plaza de la Libertad) is fantastic, they

Fiestas de San Pedro y San Pablo. Fun, fireworks and parades.

The *gigantillos y gigantones* waiting for their time to parade. Doña Jimena and El Cid to the fore.

regularly and deservedly, win the *Sampedros* tapas competition. This little plaza has on one side the palace of the Constables of Castille, whom I try to count as ancestors - looks a nice place. Also, here is the establishment of Casa Ojeda; a fabulous delicatessen on the Calle de Vitoria, a bar and outside tables on the Plaza de la Libertad and a very posh restaurant for the finest dining (book in advance) upstairs.

There is also in Burgos a small bar in a back street, the walls plastered with posters and photos of those who have been there. Guitars hang behind the bar and, of an evening, any evening, if you are lucky enough to be there, some locals will come and take an instrument. Soon a group coalesces and they are singing local songs, any songs. A beautiful tale of España. I was considering not telling you where it is, to keep it for myself, so just don't tell too many of your friends or it will lose its special ambience. Taberna Patillas is on the corner of Calle Trinas and Calle Calera.

The fiesta is many-faceted and there are *Tapas con música* moving from one Plaza to another throughout the festival with *con cante* - singing, Jazz, Rock, Salsa, Folk, Dancing - there is just so much on, everywhere! The *filas* or local marching groups all parade with their own banners and costumes.

Being part of this event is a real soul lifter, an adventure waiting for YOU.

You can get some idea of the scale of the fireworks from the flood-lit cathedral across the river. International Firework Companies compete to perform here.
The fireworks are all fired from the riverside just below the Teatro Principal.
A good place to watch the display is from is the plaza outside the Museo de la Evolución Humana.

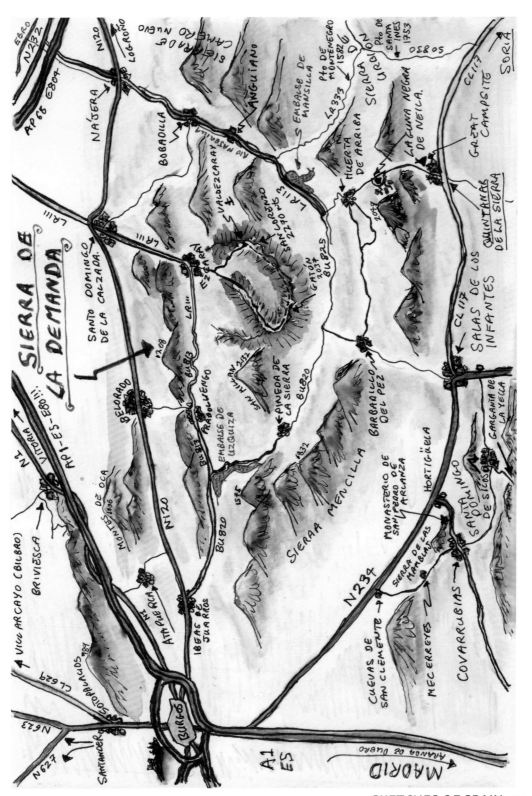

SIERRA DE LA DEMANDA

Sierra de la Demanda

I have been exploring and enjoying these mountains for seventeen years and am not tiring of them in the least. There are still nooks and crannies I haven't got into and discoveries to be made.

The mountain range lies to the east of Burgos with its highest peak being San Lorenzo at 2270 mts (just short of 7,500'). The Sierra de la Demanda and its associates; Mencilla, Urbion and Camero Nuevo cover an area about 100 km west-east and 50 km north-south. To the north is the expansive valley of the Rio Ebro which is Spain's second longest river at 928 km. The Camino de Santiago here follows the N-120 along the skirts of the Sierra. On the south side is the N-234 heading for Soria, which is at the bottom right corner of the whole extended wadge of mountains. The more easterly part of which is still awaiting my diligence.

The area has been settled since long before the Romans. On the north-western borders, at the edges of the small Montes de Oca are the caves of Atapuerca where human remains go back nearly one million years.

I guess I love this area because it is the one I have so often enjoyed. My first trip was only a week long. It takes a day just to get to the ferry port from Aberystwyth! Using Burgos as my base I had a great time exploring for the three days that I actually had in Spain, not in transit. This mountainous area provides the perfect companion to the city of Burgos. There are many different routes to explore the area.

Above Laguna Negra in the Sierra de la Demanda

On the N-120 skirting the north of the range turn in half way between Santo Domingo de la Calzada and Nájera heading for Badarán and Bobadilla (LR-312). You can also continue on and check out Nájera and there turn down the LR-113.

In 2016 (24th June) having given Martin, Phil, Steve and Al a bit of a guided tour up from Quintanar de la Sierra we stopped in Nájera to find a fiesta in progress; "The Turns" is a celebration of the festival of San Juan, with a tradition of spinning in a circle during the "Sanjuanada". The youngsters spend hours in an endless human wheel, popularly known as Las Vueltas Nájera. It certainly involved wearing ripped 'T'-shirts and shorts and pouring wine over and into each other. All very amicable though.

To continue on the route through to Quintanar over the middle of the Sierra go through Bobadilla. After about 8 km you come to Anguiano, the doorway to the mountains: A cleft guarded by huge, near vertical slabs of rock, the opening just wide enough for the narrow road, and Rio Nájerilla. 16 km later, after enjoying the winding deep valley I often stop by a small 14th century bridge that seems to lead nowhere, there is barely a track on the other side. Why was it built and if one followed its open arms where would it lead you? I wash my face in the rivers cool waters, occasionally taking a dip, though the water is always mountain cold.

Next you climb into the deep timber of the Sierra, the road twisting and doubling back on itself, never visible very far ahead At last the road turns downward towards Huerta de Arriba where there will be a welcome from

Stuffed two-headed calf in Huerta de Arriba

La Senora and *Café solo* and a plate of *aceitunas* for a break. In the way of things in Spain I once met the ex-mayor of Quintanar in a bar and on finding that I knew of the calf at Huerta he told me of the sad story of how the *señora* was widowed not long after the birth of her daughter. The early times I visited I often wondered at a feeling of sadness about her. Now her daughter is a glowing teenager. In 2016 I brought the lads here from the campsite at Quintanar. They enjoyed photographing the calf, and the refreshments. I have to say some of the roads through the Sierra were not well suited to the Harley; it kept touching its pegs down on the bends.

In 2003 it was at the end of September and though I hadn't realised it the campsite at Quintanar was about to close for the Winter. As I was riding up a car went the other way, the driver looking hard at me which I wondered about. I got to the entrance gates and they were locked. My heart sank, I had soaked gloves and damp boots. What to do and where to go? The driver of the car returned, he had guessed my destination and had turned round to come back and let me in. I asked if the little bar would be open for food later, he said it would. I realised the next day that he probably went and arranged for the girl who runs it to open up specially, just for me and a lone British cyclist who turned up later on.

On the route from Huerta over the Sierra de Neila one passes signs for the Laguna Negra de Neila. A small road winds off up into the pine forests. There are a number of lakes at the top of the Sierra with great views. In the summer months and particularly on weekends it is very popular for walks and picnics.

You could have come to Quintanar de la Sierra a number of other ways. The fastest route from Burgos is heading towards Madrid on the A1-E5 then taking the N-234 for Soria and at Salas de Los Infantes turning onto the CL-117. This way is about 85 km and will take you an hour or a bit more.

A longer route but less main road is to head out of Burgos on the N-120 for Logroño. After dodging the motorway and by-pass, turn off it at the end of Ibeas de Juarros (watch those radar controlled lights) onto the BU -820 for Pradoluengo and Ezcaray. After finding the head of the Embalse de Usquiza you will turn right for Pineda de la Sierra and drift round a lot more of the *embalse*. Some of this was a bit humpy over the last few years, but still fun, and there is every chance it might have been *obra'd* in the meantime. There are lots of places along the *embalse* where people go down and set up picnic camps by the water and enjoy themselves. Going through to Huerta de Arriba this is over 100 km and up to two and a half hours riding. Lots of fun and with alternatives possible, like going to Salas via Barbadillo or taking in Huerta de Abajo which is bit bigger and posher than Arriba despite the names: *arriba* - above, *abajo* - below.

Just inside the gates to Camping Arlanza at Quintanar is the Reception office and the staff have always been so friendly and, as in 2003, happy to go out of their way. 2016 prices were Adult €3.96, single tent €3.29, Moto €3.04; €10.29 per day. It is a lovely campsite with a 'free' area (meaning you choose where to pitch) amongst the trees beside the little river. I generally cross the small bridge with my *moto* and find a nice spot on the other side. The *cantina* does nice food, the shower block is good, there is a swimming pool and Wifi is available sitting outside your tent! They do also have chalets and bungalows.

On my trip in 2002 I arrived and found Wilf and Roy from North Wales with their 1000 cc Vincent vintage motorcycles. Wilf was 80 and Roy 75, every year they would go touring round Europe together. It was they who told me of the Necropolis nearby and lent me a rucksack to walk there.

It is a pleasant walk (3.5 km - 50 mins) in the forest or a short drive (4.5 km - 20 mins). The Necropolis of Cuyacabras dates from the 9th to the 13th centuries. There are niches cut into the sides of a big rock outcrop and body-shaped holes cut into the top of it. Apparently there were stone lids for these and a church and settlement built around it.

2016 note; the road to it has been graded after being damaged by timber trucks, at a guess. So quite rough and gravelly but easy for adventure bikes, the Harley did manage it as well. One year I amused myself by finding 'bouldering' routes over the big rock at the far side of the camping area. It had got a bit too overgrown in 2016 and though I thought about cleaning it but I was only there one night, being due in a very special little *pueblo* that I know in the Sierra. By visiting it every year, and if the villagers are tidying the verges lending a hand I have made friends and am always welcomed. That weekend there was a *cena pública* - public dinner in the Plaza Mayor. It was fantastic with 30 or more at one long table. A massive pot of *cocido* and lots of *vino* and a concert afterward.

From the bottom of the Sierra there are a couple of great places to visit not far away. Go south through Quintanar until you hit the main CL-117 road and go right for Burgos. It's not long before you arrive at the bustling little town of Salas de Los Infantes. Take the N-234 across the bridge and through the town heading towards Soria. After 4.5 km you can make a right turn onto the BU-910 for Santo Domingo de Silos. The monastery here dates from the 7th century though it has been rebuilt and is now a very good example of the Romanesque. There is a very pleasant plaza in which to sit with a coffee. To the west and a little south of the town there is a feature very well worth visiting; the Garganta de Yecla. This is a particularly spectacular 'throat'. Off the bypass roundabout take the BU-910 towards Caleruega and Aranda. After a couple of kilometres the road seems to head for an unbroken wall of rock and above massive Griffon Vultures glide to and fro

You go through two small tunnels and at the far end there is a parking area. To one side there is a small river valley that disappears into the cliff, and a gateway and steps leading down into the Garganta. The walkway is suspended within the incredibly narrow gorge. I've only been here in the summer months when it is cool, and the river merely murmurs away to itself in and out of hollowed pools. In winter spate it must be a very different place. Do mind your head because there are places where you have to duck under rock or squeeze past overhangs. When you get back up to the road you walk back through the tunnels.

You could also have come up this road from Aranda de Duero heading for Burgos or Quintanar de la Sierra or have taken a roundabout route to Lerma. I have not stayed in Lerma but the parador is said to be one of the most spectacular. Passing Lerma on the A-1 to Madrid one can see its impressive towers and facade.

If you are heading towards Burgos take in Covarrubias which is well worth the visit. At Covarrubias you can either turn left for Cuevas de San Clemente on the BU-901 which takes you through the little *pueblo* of Mecerreyes which has its own Hobbit-town. Or, take the BU-905 from Covarrubias to Hortigüela which runs through a pretty *cañón* and past the Monasterio de San Pedro de Arlanza. If you were coming up to the Sierra de la Demanda from Ayllón and the Guadarrama you could use the N-110 to El Burgo de Osma, a nice town to stop in and from where you can pick up the SO-920 going due north to San Leonardo de Yagüe.

The Cañón del Rio Lobos.

This route takes you through the Cañón del Rio Lobos. There is a pleasant looking campsite in woods by the river and a great switchback that climbs up to the northern rim where there is a *mirador* that gives great views of the *cañón* and perhaps more Griffon Vultures; it is also a good place for the colourful Azure-winged Magpie.

Going north after San Leonardo de Yagüe on a white road (SO-P-8001 and then BU-V-8229), you come to a pass - Redondo 1180 mts. Here the road splits, the right (BU-V-8225) going through Vilviestre del Pinar and the left (still the 8229) through Palacios de la Sierra. In 2016 I took the left, and after a fairly short roughish bit of road it got better, running amongst fragrant pine trees and often next to a tumbling, babbling river.

Either way when you hit the CL-117 turn right and you will shortly come to Quintanar de la Sierra.

A Long Way Round

This is mostly the route I took in 2004, (told in full in my book 'Back Roads of Spain'). But includes bits from other trips.

In 2004 the ferry brought me to Bilbao from Portsmouth. Waiting to board a ferry is always interesting. Checking out other motorbikes and having brief conversations. It often amuses me the way Brits going on a boat together seem to slip into a kind of 'Dunkirk' spirit. A middle-aged and obviously affluent couple in a big Jaguar would have ignored me in the car park of ASDA a few miles back, but here, waiting to board will strike up a friendly conversation. I have met some very interesting people over the years, a number of which I am still in contact with. In 2004, it was Cor and Jude. They drew their bike up quite close to mine and we got talking. It turned out they were on their way to Murcia where they had bought a ruin (as you do). Having spent time together that evening on board the boat we decided that we would travel together as I was heading in their general direction, though we had first nights arranged in different places. I had found a deal on www.parador.es and was booked into the Parador de Cuenca and they were staying in Molina de Aragón.

In 2004 the ferry docked at Santurtzi a bit closer to Bilbao than it does now at Zierbena. On a number of occasions I have ridden into Bilbao (in the days before SatNav) and found it pleasant as long as one stuck to the main routes and didn't end up going round and round suburbs. The Guggenheim is well signposted and once you've got down to its spectacular architecture it is easy enough to work your way back into the centre. The Guggenheim is one of those tick-boxes that is worth a detour for and Bilbao is an intriguing city. If you would like a good read about the Basques I can recommend 'The Basque History of the World' by Mark Kurlansky.

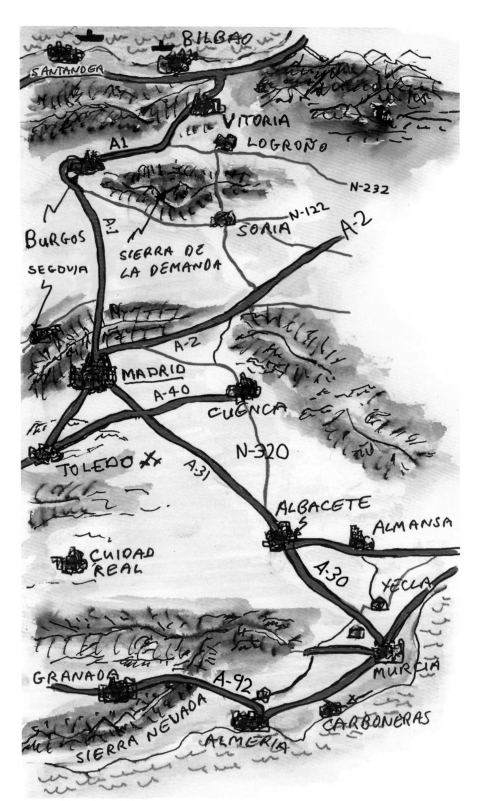

Cor had 'fettled' his Harley somewhat and said it produced something like 130 bhp. It certainly went fast, at least in straight lines. Later when I followed him I found the trail of sparks that he left from his footboards when cornering slightly alarming and certainly spectacular. We got off the motorway and onto the N-124 just before Miranda de Ebro until Haro and then the N-232 for Logroño where we turned onto the N-111 for Soria.

Just after Logroño the N-111 has one of those 10 km dead straight sections of road that seem to go on for ever to someone from this congested island. Then it enters the Valle de Iregua. This is a tributary of the Ebro and cuts between the Sierra de Camero Nuevo and Viejo (new and old) and their lesser Sierras. Both rise above 1800 mts (6,000').

In 2016 I came through to the N-111 from Nájera on the Rio Najerilla road, turning off left after Anguiano on the LR-232 which goes through Brieva de Cameros. This a great high mountain road (top pass 1720 mts I believe) with many hairpins and very scenic. After the pass there was some damage to the corners from timber lorries that required a bit of care, but it was well worth it. On the very enjoyable N-111, before you descend towards Soria you will come to the Puerto de Piqueras at 1710 mts (5,600'). The road goes into a tunnel, just before there is a sign saying 'CON ALTURA EXCESIVA DESVÍO POR PTO. PIQUERAS' directing high vehicles onto the old

Just below the Puerto de Piqueras.

road. It is well worth taking it. No traffic, great views and I had a *corzo* - roe deer bound across the road ahead of me.

Unfortunately after Soria the N-111 has recently been sanitized into the A-15 motorway. At Medinacelli you get on the A2-E90 southward for a few kilometres and after a tunnel under the Puerto de Alcolea you hit the junction for Alcolea del Pinar. There are two ways I have gone from here to Cuenca, both good fun. In 2004 because of where Cor and Jude were heading we hung a left onto the N-211 heading south-east to Molina de Aragón where after a beer and snack in a small square we parted company for the time being. They went on down the main road but I cut back south and slightly west on the back roads to Cuenca.

The CM-210 took me past the Parque Natural del Alto Tajo and on through the Serranía de Cuenca. A typically expansive and diverse back-road. Gorges, tiny villages, dusty fields and the great blue sky, rushing rivers and ancient monuments. After Beteta it gets more fun as one enters a *desfiladero*, literally a defile or gorge for around 10 kms. At Cañamares (which has a campsite that looks reasonable though I haven't tried it out), I continued south to La Frontera where I got onto a yet smaller road, the CUV-9116 which continues south through fields, a typical back road, smooth, plenty of variety in straights and corners and very largely empty of traffic, so you can enjoy yourself at whatever speed you like. After Mariana one joins the CM-2105 and the Rio Júcar. After a few kilometres I saw a sign for La Ciudad Encantada. My translation being 'the Enchanted City', I decided to explore it the next day but went on into the gorge-split Cuenca, with its *casas colgadas* - 'hanging houses', and the welcoming Parador.

There is another route from Alcolea which I have used, going westward on the E-90 for 16 kms and then turning off onto the GU-298 which perhaps becomes the GU-929 and then the CM-2018 bringing you down to Priego which is close to Cañamares.

In 2007 I came down from Ayllón a little further west and used the N-204 off the E-90. This was a slightly faster road and where it goes round and across the Embalse de Entrepeñas has some great views. You end up at Sacedón and can take the N-320 down to Cuenca.

These yellow and white back roads are for me the very essence of adventuring in Spain. So many sights and smells and vistas. Little *pueblos*, all alike but different. Stopping in cool village bars for some simple refreshment, giving a nod to the *viejos* sitting sun-warmed on a roadside bench watching the world go by. Made their day with a bit of luck.

I think that time in 2004 we must have come off the ferry between 9 and 10am, had coffee near Vitoria and a late lunch in Molina with me arriving at the Parador around 6pm. A pretty easy 8 hours on the road, 550 kms (340 miles). I didn't arrive tired out but buzzing with all that I had seen and experienced. A good part of that was because of using the back roads. Travelling at good average speeds and yet in a very relaxed way. With hardly any traffic one can really look around, stop to birdwatch if one wants. Even go back over a particularly good bit of road just for fun. A *tranquilo viaje* – a journey with tranquillity.

Cuenca

Cuenca is an engaging little city, the more modern part spreads out from the foot of low mountains which are cut by a deep gorge. The main old town is on top and along the very edge of the gorge. The famous *casas colgadas* are large wooden balconies that are built out over the cliff edge. There is a footbridge that crosses the gorge to where the Parador is perched on the other side. The Catedral de Santa María y San Julián de Cuenca is surprisingly small but worth a visit and since I was last there a new Science museum, the Museo de las Ciencias de Castilla La Mancha has been opened and looks very interesting. There is also a museum of Spanish Abstract Art - Museo de Arte Abstracto Español which is housed in the *casas colgadas*. With the confined size of the old town it is a great place to have a lazy day sightseeing.

The Parador is one of my favourites. It is in what was the Monastery of San Pablo which was established in 1523 although the building was really only finished in its present form in the 18th century. It has a very restful air, the central cloister of the building giving a sense of spaciousness. The restaurant (very good) was the refectory and still has its coffered ceiling. Close by is the rock called La Sultana. The sense of the closeness of history is very strong, the iron footbridge to the city was erected in 1895 but rests on the stone pillars of the bridge built by Juan del Pozo in 1543 which

though extant had become unsafe. Back to Visigothic and Roman times the *Conquenses* (from Cuenca) have had a curious reputation for being unruly and rebellious but also very welcoming. Apparently a local saying is *"Cortesía no resta valor"* - "Courtesy does not detract from courage".

That first time I arrived on my motorbike, hot, dusty and sweaty I was met with great courtesy. No slightly sideways looks as one might get in a posh English Hotel. "Of course you can leave your *moto* just outside where it says 'No Parking'. Do you want a hand with your bags?" The bathroom alone was nearly as big as my living room at home. The bedroom enormous, and when I opened the shutters I had a view of the footbridge and the *casas colgadas*.

Going back for something else off my bike I spotted this glorious praying mantis on the wall which I realised was laying eggs. It was so still and other-worldly, just like the Arab lady still watching over the monastery.

In 2016 I came back to the Parador after walking the town to find the central courtyard busy with diners being serenaded by a violin played by a young lady. I got a glass of *vino tinto* and enjoyed a grand end to the day. Mia Jimena was playing Bach cello suites, a Telemann Fantasias and Mozart arias. La Sultana listened, peering down into the courtyard.

Perhaps there is some magic in these wild lands that

The Parador as a balmy evening soothes the traveller.

makes imagination flourish in relation to natural forms. Don Quixote is not alone. Go to the Enchanted City!

There is a circular route to the Ciudad Encantada that you can take using the CM-2104 and 5, which adds nicely to the trip and on the way round it is worth stopping at the Ventano del Diablo (Devil's Window).

The Ciudad is interesting and at times bizarre, though not what I had expected. It consists of a maze of weathered rock forms with sometimes appropriate, though often, names that need a bit of Don Quixote's imagination attached.

Mar de Piedra, El Teatro, El Diplodocus, Cara del Hombre, El Perro and El Cocodrillo y El Elefante.

Here I had one of those experiences that are so much a part of touring. Whilst waiting for the place to open I got talking to a New Zealand couple with a camper van, that progressed to coffee and biscuits, and we chatted as we went around the Ciudad. Afterwards we parted, never to meet again, but all enriched.

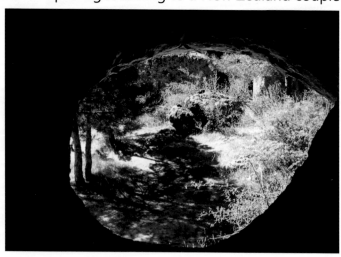

Leaving Cuenca I took a white road off the N-320 to skirt Albacete via La Roda. I stopped to bite on a hunk of bread and gnaw the end off a *chorizo*. I got a text message from Jude and decided to switch direction and meet them in Almansa. Looking at the map (see, you couldn't do that easily with your SatNav), for a back-road route I spotted the CM-3218, a very windy road that follows the Rio Júcar. That many bends showing on a 1/350 000 map means FUN! It is! A snaking ride, often needing first gear to ride round blind, tight corners and under rock overhangs that have one instinctively ducking. At times the road seems barely wide enough for four wheels, though there is probably a local bus coming through every day.

<u>Rio Júcar</u>

It is easy to miss the many cave - *cueva* houses in the *cañón* walls.

Notice the doorway in the cliff.

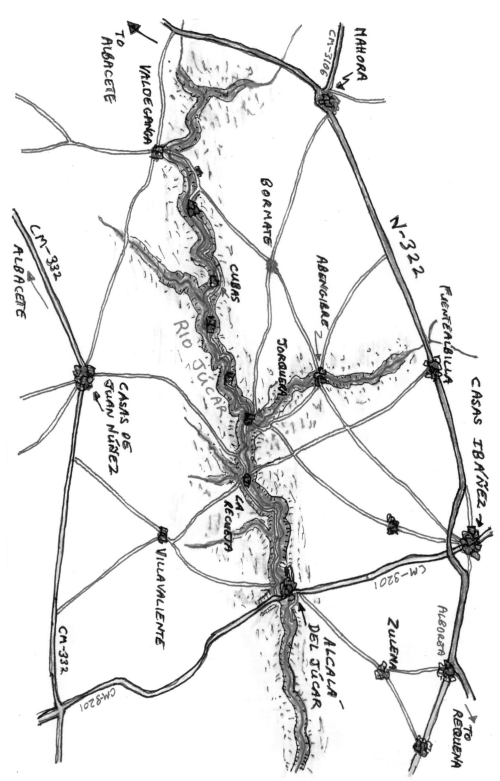

A glance at the cliffs across the *cañón* at an intriguing feature that seems not quite natural is at first no more than puzzling. Stop, look closer, and there is a fascinating human dimension, square dark windows or doorways. This whole region has characteristic limestone geological forms. It is very interesting the way in which humans have used the geology for defence and in creating cool protected living spaces.

After a little while one comes upon the *pueblo* of Cubas, squeezed between the *cañón* walls and the river, most of the buildings including the church are sheltered by an overhang and built into the cliff.

A bit further on where the Rio Abengibre joins the Rio Júcar is Jorquera, one of the most spectacular towns I have 'happened' upon in my quest for back road adventures. The photo on the next page doesn't really do justice to the way it is perched on a virtual island of rock around 80 mts (260') above the *cañón* floor. At one time the subsidiary of the Júcar the Abengibre must have broken through a narrow wall of rock to join the Júcar about 800 mts further upstream, creating this island of rock.

Cubas church

Can you imagine the delight of the first people who found this natural defensive position?

Further on I came upon a place where a corner in the road had been removed by a digger, in the bluff were these strange triangular openings. I had to investigate. What they were for I have absolutely no idea. I was able to crawl in one and come out the other after going perhaps fifteen feet into the hillside. The sides seemed to show the marks of some kind of hand adze used to dig them out.

Just before Alcalá del Júcar I stopped when I noticed what looked like more windows in the cliffs across the river. Not only were there many windows there, but also a balcony and tables and writing on the cliff; 'Cuevas del Diablo'! Well a restaurant called the Devil's Caves sounded very interesting.

In 2004 I didn't have the time to try and find the way to it. In 2007 I tried following signs toward it and came to a fork in the steep lane up. Both directions had signs for the *cuevas*. I took the left hand one which got narrower and steeper, then there was a section of those long low and sloping steps. I thought I must be close and have seen cars drive up this sort of thing elsewhere. It was late morning and the town seemed empty. Anybody with a brain would have got off and walked up to check it out. I didn't and when I got to the top of the set of steps I knew I was in trouble; to my left a steep staircase upward (to the *cuevas*), ahead sloping steps downward. "Oh, s-dear!" I tried to walk the bike back down the way I had come but the front wheel slid when braked, suffice to say I dropped it. I was having real difficulty trying to get it up again as it was too close to a sidewall. Luckily the first people I had seen came along, a son and father who grabbed a hold and got me back to the flat space at the top of the steps. What they thought of this daft *guiri* I don't want to think, though they were very friendly about it.

Now I took the time to have a look at how I was going to get out. I couldn't turn the bike round so it was going to have to be down the steps ahead. I was in a right sweat and bother by this time, embarrassed as hell and the air temperature was heading up in the thirties... The steps down were shorter steeper and deeper. Most looked just feasible except for the last one which looked to be enough of a drop to ground the bike. There was not a brick or piece of wood to be found. Luckily I had a strong plastic water bottle, this placed below the step was just enough. Even so it was a very hairy few moments. I headed straight off to Albacete to meet up with

Nick from Bristol who I had met on the ferry and travelled with the first couple of days, he was staying with a Spanish friend who knew where there was a Moto Guzzi dealer who was able to fix my bent brake pedal. The Cuevas del Diablo are now a museum, which I believe costs €3 to get into.

2016. After getting new photos of the *cañón* I arrived in Alcalá, I thought I might try again to get to the Cuevas. I turned up the steep road into the town, got about 10 mts and bottled out! The way onward was even steeper, the roadway was now polished marble cobbles with a glass like slipperyness, it was mid 30 degrees and I didn't know where I was going to be that night. I thought about parking and walking up, but knew it would probably take a couple of hours out of the day. With an old lady watching me from her terrace I turned around, nearly dropping the bike again on the slippy surface. I'm going to have to break the jinx of the Cuevas del Diablo one of these years!

SO there you go, an adventure to beat me to!

Breathing a sigh of relief I decided to get across the country and see Guadalupe and Monfragüe, which had long been on a list of 'to do's'. In Albacete a guy had me follow him to get on the right road for Manzanares (150 km) when all the signposts were for Bailén which is (270 km)!

Have you rode the vast plains of La Mancha? Before you a distance that is hard to encompass? A distant haze keeps the horizon and hidden mountain ranges secret. Though one is riding, for the moment under clear skies and in a steady dry heat, ahead there are dark grey, threatening, towering, jellyfish-clouds trailing almost black tentacles of stinging rain. Some are lit with lightning. One feels small and alone, but also intensely alive. At times I am riding like Richard III, hunched against a long, ill blowing crosswind.

That day I rode 650 km, from Cuenca to Herrara del Duque 100 km west of Ciudad Real, taking in the *cañón* of the Rio Júcar as I went round Albacete. I somehow passed the jellyfish unstung, my nostrils filled with that scent of rain on dry earth, or going through a *pueblo* that had recently been inundated by a cloudburst. By the time I got to Herrara I was getting a bit weary. My first pass into the town found no hostals or hotels, a typical dusty dry town of narrow lanes. Now I was feeling the day's travel and a sense of despair, but back on the main road and further round the town... 'HOTEL', but on closer inspection, obviously closed up. Last chance, turn back into the town. A short distance and I see a sign 'Hostal Carlos I', it seemed open. Quick, park bike by the nearest pavement table. Let's hope... My initial reception in the bar was a bit frosty compounded by the proprietors throat problem, which required a local sitting at the bar to translate, but as my mangled Spanish took hold, got better, and better. So I got a nice room.

After a shower I took a place at a roadside table, got some wonderful *sepia* - cuttlefish, and watched the way this little world works. Here, every passer-by whether on foot or loud music-ked car acknowledges the people seated at the street tables, every passer-by is known and greeted. I got to share drinks with the local carpenter and bemoan the troubles of self-employment. Later I sat on my balcony as above me bats joined the swallows and martins hawking for insects in the hot air. I slept well that night.

In 2004 I met up again with Cor and Jude under Almansa's impressive castle-crested rock and together we rode on to Yecla where we found the delightful Hotel Avenida, nice rooms, good price, in the middle of town. Best of all a lock-up garage with direct access to the rooms. Yecla is a quiet, pleasant, fairly industrial town of a little over 30,000 inhabitants. Yet another 'back road' town that just gives you so much SPAIN. We were trying to find our way to the Hotel when we were instructed by a *policía local* to go down a one way street the wrong way, 'carefully'!

In Spain, so often common sense and pragmatism is the norm, the natural way for officials to act, as long as **you** have the right attitude.

I have been told that the sculpted rocks of Monte Arabí about 15 km to the north-west are worth a visit. Yecla is not on any major route though the N-344 goes on to Jumilla and to Murcia itself, the provincial capital. Just try and fit Yecla in to your desperate race for Marbella.

After visiting Cor and Jude's house in the little Sierra del Carche I took a bit of a mad route to Tabernas. To start with I cut back to the N-344 and Jumilla. Although with typical industrial areas and urban sprawl spread out around the town, the older part and the remaining part of the Castillo perched on top of the rocky hill above the town make it a reasonable place to take a break. The not far distant mountains seem closer than they are, in the harder southern light, the land already showing the signs of far less precipitation.

I didn't want to get sucked into the built-up areas and motorways of Murcia and so picked on Cehegín to keep my distance from the Costa. I got onto the C-3314, well that's what it was called back then. NOW it is called the RM-714, an example of why updating maps is a good idea but also the limitations of a SatNav; if you can see the *pueblos* you want to go through, you can pick the right road no matter what the number. Writing this, I often check with Google maps as well, sometimes finding yet other numbers. The road follows the wide valley of the Rambla del Judio – I'm not sure I want to know what the Jew was doing in the 'dry riverbed'. A couple of kilometres to either side run low mountain spines, the Sierra del Molar and Larga. I cruised the back road at a pretty steady 100 kmph (60 mph), as fast as I would have been going on the motorways but without the hassle. And I can take time to birdwatch, and just enjoy the 'go-ing'. I used to think that Spanish petrol was of a better quality as my fuel consumption was always so much better than in the UK, eventually realising it is the steady and far more relaxed riding. The road gentled me along to Calasparra which of course has its Castillo above it. About 5 km to the north there is the Santuario de la Esperanza built into the cliff it sits against.

Next I passed by Cehegín, and although I know the route I had planned to take (highlighted on the map) I have a distinct feeling that I didn't follow it exactly. I'm pretty sure I came out at Vélez Rubio though whether I went down the RM-370 to Puebla de Don Fadrique and then A-317 or some other way I don't know. Likewise my planned route went west on the A-91 (was N-342) to Chirivel before cutting south to Albox. Then through the Sierra de los Filabres to Los Yesos on the N-340.

NOTE! When adventuring, mark up a map of where you actually went, highlight good stops etc. After the next day's adventures what you thought you'd remember till you got round to writing it down, is gone.

Tabernas is where the mis-named 'Spaghetti Western' film sets are. Okay, the Director Sergio Leone was Italian. The sets 'Mini-Hollywood' and 'Fort Bravo' were the main point of that 2004 trip. I was, and still am writing a series of historical novels set in the 1800's largely in Arizona. Tabernas is a bit closer and cheaper than going to the USA.

From Yecla to Tabernas the shortest route would be 240 km (150 miles), I managed to notch up nearly 480 km that day. Not all of it intentional. I had tried to pre-book the Hospederia del Desierto (very close to the Almeria racing circuit), but had been told it wasn't possible. For some reason I thought they were probably just being cautious and that when I got there they would find me something. No such luck! It was a special Saturday

for getting married and it was packed. "Anywhere to camp?" *Nada*. So, somewhat tiredly and forlornly, I headed back onto the road. Reaching Tabernas itself I saw from the road a sign painted on a building 'HOTEL'. It didn't look too promising but after a trip round the village that showed no other candidates I drew up and tried the door. After a while I was shown to a very small room. Oh well, it's an experience, take what comes. After attempting a shower, (broken) like the rather smelly toilet, I lay down for a rest. I found myself being eaten by small but extremely aggressive biting flies. Enough is enough, I'd rather sleep in a ditch. I quickly packed, made vague excuses, and legged it! I now think it may well have been more of a brothel than a hotel. What an escape. As I have mentioned in the Really Useful Stuff at the end of the book; a 'club', 'disco', 'dancing' or 'hotel' right on the outskirts of a town, or a field or two away from it with a big weedy car park is probably a brothel.

Sixty-odd miles later as full-dark settled across the Mediterranean I was putting my tent up on a beach north of Carboneras. This was not quite as simple as it sounds. I had made the mistake of picking up my Michelin map in a second-hand bookshop and it was well out of date, the roads I thought I was riding were not the ones on the map, same area but going different routes. I had gone looking for campsites or hostals, went through Sorbas and then got sucked onto the A7-E15 that my map didn't know about. I had to get off the *autovia* to check where I was going and the slip road was headed for Carboneras. When I got there my 'COSTAS' alarm rang. 'Hmm, fish and chip bars, UK number plates, get me out of here!' For some reason I went north. A nice road parallel to the sea. Seeing various dirt cut-offs that led to the beach, and the odd VW Combi down there obviously setting up for the night; I thought 'Why not?' So I did.

Taking off my helmet as dusk fell I was aware of that wonderful sense of

'adventuring'. 'Here I am, miles from where I should be...' BUT, so what, the air is heavy with salt of the Mediterranean, the surf is a soft susurration, and I am at the end of a fantastic day's travel. A dozen years on, that moment is still with me. I sneaked down to the sea in the dark, and bathed naked in the warm Mediterranean. My supper was rather meagre as I hadn't expected to be wild camping. Two bites of rather sweaty *chorizo* and a swig of warm water. But I slept the sleep of the 'just', and tired *caballero*.

In the morning I retraced my steps to the film sets. Both were somewhat odd collections of bits of Western townships. It's all good fun though; actors stroll around and look mean and eventually act out a scenario of bank robbery, pursuit, capture and a hanging. Lots of blanks being fired and horses cantered. After my research activities I was able to get a room in the Hostal Calatrava (€25), part of the Hospederia del Desierto.

The next day was 'the ride' of the whole 2004 trip. Exhausting, exhilarating, seemingly endless. Somehow the day seemed to stretch itself as I rode, to encompass the distance covered. A distance not only measured in turns of my wheels but also in both history and geography. A journey from the Moorish, 'African' landscape of the Almeria desert, beating north and west against the receding tide of the Moorish conquest and ending in the mist-soaked Sierra de Gredos. Through which the God-armed Christian knights brought the *Reconquista*.

First of all though came the road to Granada, over 140 km of sweeping hot tarmac and exploding views of the Sierra Nevada reaching up to 3478 mts (11,411') and holding high the most southerly permanent snow in Europe. Coming round a long bend after passing the Puerta Lobo (wolf-pass) I found the city spread out before me in the distance. I eagerly looked for any sign of La Alhambra, the fabled Moorish citadel of many awed descriptions. When I finally found it I could see nothing but a long, low red-brown wall. And it was fully-booked! They only allow a certain number in at any time in order to preserve something of its fabled magic. Book in advance is the answer, as I did 2010 and 2016.

<u>Granada</u>

Alhambra, June 2010. There was still quite a lot of snow on the Sierra Nevada though the city below was above thirty degrees. I had found a small room in the Hotel Guadalupe, right opposite the entrance to the Alhambra which was ideal for getting in as soon as it opened.

Alhambra, March 2016. My wife and I had an early breakfast in the excellent Hotel Mirador Arabeluj and made the short walk to the Alhambra

entrance. By using the card I had paid for them online I was able to get our tickets quickly from a machine (situated at the far side of the Entrance Pavilion by the Groups office). Thereby, avoiding the already extensive (9am) queue to collect tickets. Being early is well worth it as we went straight into the Nasrid Palace and where able to get in without queuing and enjoy the Palace without too many tour groups around us. We were lucky with good weather and certainly benefited from it being earlier in the season.

It is perhaps a little hard to feel the spirit

View of Granada from our room in the Hotel Mirador Arabeluj (ask for the view when you book).

of the place with all the groups of tourists being shepherded round, told what to look at, what to see. But sometimes one can sit in a quiet corner and reach for the minds of the emirs and sultans who created these intricate water gardens, areas of peace and seclusion amongst the rambling palaces. Find a window that gives a framed view of the sierra or a doorway that beckons the mind to the courtyard beyond. Catch the smell of orange blossom, honeysuckle and cedar.

Sitting for a short while and doing a simple sketch gives time to appreciate the intricacies of Moorish architecture. The Alhambra is justly a World Heritage site.

We had arrived from Córdoba on the ALSA coach, this was very comfortable and well driven. We were given a cake and bottle of water

each on boarding and there was a film shown. My wife doesn't generally like coach travel but found it fine and like me, enjoyed the scenery. The alternative train journey would have taken the same time and cost a lot more, it also involved a change at Antequera. The Granada bus station is a little way out of town but it was easy to catch the SN1 into the centre, getting off at the *Catedral* (Cathedral). €1.20 (each) gave us any number of city buses in an hour so we could have made our way straight to the Plaza de Isabel La Católica and caught the C3 bus up to the Alhambra. Instead we enjoyed a few hours wandering the streets around the cathedral, having drinks in small plazas and generally being good tourists.

In 2004 I headed out of Granada for the next great Spanish city on my list, Córdoba, about 160 km away.

<u>Córdoba</u>

In 2004, I pulled off onto a wide pavement close to the river, within sight of the great Cathedral - La Mezquita. Across the road was an inviting bar and when I asked the owner if my bike would be safe where it was, whilst I went to La Mezquita. She told me to bring it over in front of the bar, she would keep an eye on it for me. So typical of the openness and helpfulness a little effort with language brings.

The Puente Romano and the whole riverside area has now been made pedestrian friendly without car parking although there are areas where you can park *motos*. This makes the totally pedestrian bridge a part of the riverside *paseo*. My previous visits had been somewhat fleeting so spending a number of days here with my wife was a pleasant change. I had time to sit and sketch and to enjoy birdwatching from the Puente

Romana. It was exciting to see Nightingales, Night Herons, Great White and Cattle Egrets on the river and its margins.

Getting a reasonable street map is a good idea, that way you can mark down good restaurants and places you want to go back to amongst the maze of tiny streets that make up the Barrio de la Juderia - Jewish Quarter. This is right behind the Moorish mosque that is now the Catholic Cathedral! I would not advise entering any of this maze with a vehicle, even a motorbike, they are stuffed with pedestrians and largely cobbled, the chances of getting lost or stuck are high.

La Mezquita is a wonderful place, despite embodying in one way the war of religion. A Christian cathedral squatting in a Muslim mosque. It seems to me this illustrates a fascinating facet of Spain and the Spanish. Much is made of the great Reconquista, the God blessed re-conquest of Iberia from the Moorish invaders (who had been there for 800 years) and a *hidalgo*, a noble gentleman guaranteed he had no Arab blood. The battles were bloody, and in the end all Arabs and Jews were supposed to have been thrown out, killed or converted. The dreaded, cruel Spanish Inquisition was created to make sure of the new purity of religion in Spain.

And yet, so much of the architecture and ways of living were assimilated. The great iconic El Cid fought on both sides, and for himself; Rodrigo Díaz de Vivar (1043 – 1099) was a Castilian. In fact it was the Moors who called him El Cid ('Lord' from the Arabic *sayyid*), the Christians called him El Campeador (the Champion). He was born in Vivar, a town near

Burgos in the Cathedral of which is his tomb.

You do not have to book to get in to La Mezquita. But you do need to get your tickets from the ticket office across the Court of Oranges before joining the queue to get in. You are likely to have to show the contents of any bag. There are not really any noticeable restrictions on the number of people let in, so getting there early can give you a better experience. It is one of those spaces that are best to experience rather than try to encapsulate with photographs which just cannot give the sense of space, or repetition, or of the feeling of timelessness that pervades it. I noticed how the varied marble columns are all polished from child hand height to adult, ages of human sweat and oils now a part of the fabric of the building.

La Mezquita has a sense of peace, perhaps the ghosts of all the Christians and Muslims that have worshipped here down the ages have infused the very stones. It may be that this is the key to why I enjoy it more than the Alhambra. The former is essentially a palace for an elite ruling class, its peacefulness comes from power over the masses and their exclusion.

Particularly in the south and east of Spain there are fiestas dedicated to the great religious conflict. Fiestas de Moros y Christianos (Alcoy inland north of Alicante has a great one) events happen from big cities to tiny villages. There is great pride in the year-long meetings and preparations of the *filas* or parade groups with their handmade individual costumes and often a small band. All ages are represented. There is a fairly equal preponderance

of Moors and Christians and though traditionally the Christians win any enactment it seems to me that these events are a typical Spanish confection with more than a hint of subversion. A celebration in fact, of the complicated mix that makes Spain so fascinating.

These gorgeously dressed *filas* were in a village of probably no more than a couple of hundred houses, though I expect the surrounding area contributed.

There is a story of a princess of the Alhambra who loved the sight of the snows on the Sierra Nevada. She married the prince of Córdoba but became sad as she could no longer see the snows. So the prince had the sierra of Córdoba planted with almond trees so that in the spring the mountains would be dusted with white blossom.

The Moors had public baths and great libraries, were pretty tolerant of other religions and they brought Aristotle back into the light. Towards the end of their rule though, they became as restrictive as the Christians. No religious fundamentalism is really good for its society in my opinion.

My wife and I very much enjoyed the Alcázar, entering as soon as it opened to avoid the crowds. Having seen all the rooms, we walked the gardens and just sat peaceably listening to the sound of the fountains and wishing we had brought a picnic whilst I made sketch and notes (below) in my journal. I had in my pocket an orange from one of the ubiquitous trees of the city. I do not have a sweet tooth and enjoy eating sloe's and lemons and I enjoyed my 'marmalade' orange. They are pretty sharp but certainly not poisonous as I have seen suggested.

Casa de las Cabezas (house of heads) a 'historical house' about 200 mts from La Mezquita is worth a visit to get an idea of how the Moors and then Christians lived in Al Andalus.

This 2016 visit to Córdoba, Granada and Sevilla was for our 30th Wedding Anniversary and was for me different from my normal way of experiencing Spain. We flew to Madrid and then took the AVE, the high-speed train to Córdoba. There we based ourselves for the week. The train was superb, the transfer from the Airport (Terminal 4 because we flew Iberia) to Atocha bus and train station easy enough. Though on the way back we did get a €30

Puente Romana

(standardised fare) taxi from Atocha to Terminal 1 as we were a bit short of time and the connections to Terminals 1,2 and 3 are not quite as good. Spanish public transport is of a very high standard and very well used. The T4 to Atocha suburban train was free because of our AVE tickets which I had bought and printed out in advance. I was unable to buy the ALSA tickets from Córdoba to Granada though due to a requirement for a five number post code, this may get sorted in the future. Our AVE tickets, the cheapest, were unchangeable and non-refundable which could have been a problem if we had needed to change plans at all.

The Parador in Córdoba was reasonable at €80 per night (you pay for the room not the number of guests) and it was nice after the day's travel to relax and eat on the terrace with a view over the city. The rooms were as excellent as always with the paradors. We could have paid a bit more for a balcony view above the terrace but were happy with what we had overlooking the entrance area where a fountain splished and splashed through the night. When we returned from one night in Granada we stayed in the Hostal Alcazar 1 for two nights. Close to the Alcazar and the Barrio de la Judería and now we were in the swing of things, it was good to be close to all the sites and the restaurants. The hostal is idiosyncratic but the room we had (No1) was very reasonable and the owner Don Fernando is a hoot. The room we had in the Hotel Zaida in Sevilla was nice but I gained the impression that

as with the perfectly good Hostal La Fuente back in Córdoba there were rooms that might not have been so good. They were all good value in our opinion. Both hostals in Córdoba allowed us to leave the large rucksack and another bag with them a day in advance of our check-in, so we only took what we needed to Granada and Sevilla.

La Herradura - Plaza Alhondiga 30/3/16.

Sevilla

Another city I have not visited on *moto*. My wife and I came here from Córdoba on the excellent AVE high speed train. We walked into the city from the Santa Justa station, arriving at the Parasol (above) after a kilometre and a half, about twenty minutes. It was then I realised I didn't have my camera. We had stopped for a coffee when we came out from the station so I went back and asked if I had left it there and logged it as possibly left on the train at the RENFE Customer Services. They were very efficient but neither came up with anything. At one or other I guess it was stolen. I was surprised as in my experience which has included people leaving cameras and passports on bar tables the staff have always kept them safe until picked up. But then I guess Sevilla is a big city and one needs to be a bit more careful. Although the loss of a number of photos from Córdoba was a blow, luckily I still had my tablet to take photos with and my sketchbook. The Parasol is amazing, sculpture and architecture well combined, with a metro station beneath it and a bar in the canopy as well as a viewing platform. Sevilla is a lively city with so much to see that our one night and parts of days either side barely

scratched the surface but was highly enjoyable. My wife liking it above Córdoba and Granada, whereas I preferred the smallest - Córdoba. From the Parasol we moved into the smaller, older streets and within ten minutes had found the Hotel Zaida. It is quite large with 26 rooms and certainly all the main areas are pleasant with a very Moorish decoration and ambiance. From here it was only about 15 minutes walk to most things we wanted to see. Foremost of these was the Alcázar. It opens at 9.30 am and it is worth being there before that because even in early April queues formed very quickly, for pre-booked as well as 'on the door'. There is much to enjoy,

and as with the Alhambra, wonder at the skills and attitude to life of the Moorish rulers who created such wonderful gardens and then the Christian kings who took it over and developed their own style, that was still very much informed by the inherited architecture. Pedro the Cruel of Castille in particular, who in the 1360's did a lot of rebuilding and enlarging. He did use Moorish craftsmen and although there are Gothic and renaissance parts they are generally harmonious. The gardens are beautiful, but unfortunately for us it began to drizzle curtailing our enjoyment. The photo on the next page is of Los Baños de Doña María de Padilla, the baths of the mistress of Pedro the Cruel and are also a rainwater reservoir.

The Cathedral is massive and worth the contrast of

architecture and function.

We wanted to see some Flamenco but were unfortunately unable to get a ticket for the show at the Museo del Baile Flamenco which would have been the best. We did see some Flamenco in a restaurant in Córdoba but it was rather formulaic and touristy.

Going up the Torre del Oro or taking a riverside walk or a boat trip will give one a sense of the size of the city.

There is much else to see and Sevilla deserves a longer stay.

Cordoba to the Sierra de Gredos

Back in 2004 I headed out of Córdoba up the N-432 which goes to Badajoz. After 50 km I turned off onto the N-502 though on the map it is yellow and is pretty much a back road, then onto the A-422, winding through a changing land, the vast dryness and expanses of Andalucía gave gradual way to the more intricate and varied lands of Extremadura. Mountains and *embalses*, this part of Spain is often forgotten, a child forever ostracised from the fire of Andalucía and the aristocracy of Castilla. Extremadura seems without the nationalism or champions of the Catalans or Basques. But it is always there, has always been there, quietly working its high rocky way along the backbone of Iberia. A tough, quietly independent land. They use granite fence posts!

I think at Cabeza del Buey (head of the ox), I turned left to enjoy the Sierra de Tiros on the EX-104 to Castuera before turning back northward to cross the Embalse de la Serena. I crossed the main N-430 and followed the much smaller N-502 for Talavera de la Reina crossing another small mountain range, the tail of the Sierra de Guadalupe. See my 2016 visit to Guadalupe

and Monfragüe. Near Talavera, in 2008 whilst visiting Peninsular War battlefields for a proposed guided tour, I tried to identify the salient points of the battle in July 1809 when Sir Arthur Wellesley (Duke of Wellington) forced the French under Marshal Victor to retreat. There is now an impressive monument to the battle.

Sierra de Gredos

The next mountain range north of Talavera is the Sierra de Gredos, 2,592 mts (over 8,500') and that day it was gathering a dark cloak of steel and iron clouds. North of Arenas de San Pedro on the now upgraded N-502 I came to Mombeltrán and with the light fading I saw a sign for a Hostal and camping. My welcome was genuine, yes, a room, yes, you can put your *moto* under the little outside roof where the kids are laughing over an old table-football game. When settled at the bar I received free tapas with the schooner of beer the barman fixed me. A simple, but unbelievably satisfying *tortilla* and *pan* supper. It seemed much more than a day ago that I had left the Hostal at Tabernas in the 45° *desierto*. Over 700 km (450 miles). Tired, yes, but also exhilarated and full to the brim with experience. The next morning there was a light mist, which came and went as I climbed toward the pass of the Puerto del Pico 1352 mts (4,437'), where for a while it drizzled. At first I was irritated, and riding rather gingerly, but then as the clouds part I gained magnificent views of the mountains and it all made sense. Without the blindfold of cloud I couldn't have had the sudden revelation. And on the twisting mountain road, the dampness seemed to accentuate the heady scents of pine and rosemary, which along with broom clothed what I could see of the roadsides.

The N-520 criss-crosses and cuts through long paved and sloping steps.

The remains of a Roman road; in the mist I imagine the legions marching, the length of each 4 or 5 metre 'step', carefully engineered to suit their marching rhythm.

I passed over the Sierra de Villafranca at the Puerto de la Peña Negra 1909 mts (6,263') in thick cloud with visibility down to yards, however as I wound my way down I dropped suddenly clear and found a huge swathe of country

in bright sun, textured by the shadows of drifting clouds, and a Red Kite drifting gracefully. I hurried on down flitting left and right to the beating pace of the road's hairpins. A bird flitted across in front of me, dazzling me with flashes of blue, green and tawny red. I slammed on the brakes and ripped off my helmet, almost dropping the bike in my hurry to get at my binoculars. First I was aware of the penetrating, purring, chirruping calls, and then the fast flying shapes of a flock of twenty or more Bee-eaters, all

Puerto de la Peña Negra, at Angeles Bar.

around me their jewel-like colours shimmering. To ice the ornithological cake; a huge Black Vulture was drifting across the face of the mountains.

In 2016 I came this way after leaving the Parador de Gredos on the AV-941. Piedrahita was not signposted off the AV-932, it said La Herguijela instead, a tiny *pueblo*. I found a new development at the top of the pass. A small building housing a bar, and by it take-off and landing strips for paragliders. It is presided over by the friendly Angeles Yesa who makes her own excellent jams and pastries. I sketched as I breakfasted. I left Angeles as a number of minibuses and a coach arrived with assorted high-flying *aficionados*. I was lucky to get my bike out before it was double parked against the cliff edge. I poured myself down the switchbacks towards Piedrahita. Somewhere in the next 20 km I decided on a detour before I got to Ávila. About 9 km out of Piedrahita I turned off onto the AV-P-507. Shortly I took a detour because I saw a sign for Garganta de los Hornos. I trickled up a pretty little valley until I came to the edge of the *pueblo*, most of the houses seemed to be falling down and I decided to turn around where I could. Back on the main road I continued on towards San Martín de la Vega del Alberche. A nice wind up to the Puerto de Chia - 1,663 mts, and then down to the town. I was now in a wonderful high plateau between the Sierra de la Paramera and the Sierra de Gredos. A pretty bare plain with a few poplars along the river and around the villages, but with a kind of grandeur imparted by the mountain ridges to either side. It had a feeling of a secret place, one rarely visited. Certainly I did get some astonished looks as I slowly cruised through the bare lands scented by bright yellow broom, interspersed with wheat or barley fields. Occasionally the road would dive into a small *barranca* that would be so heavy with honeysuckle I could almost taste it.

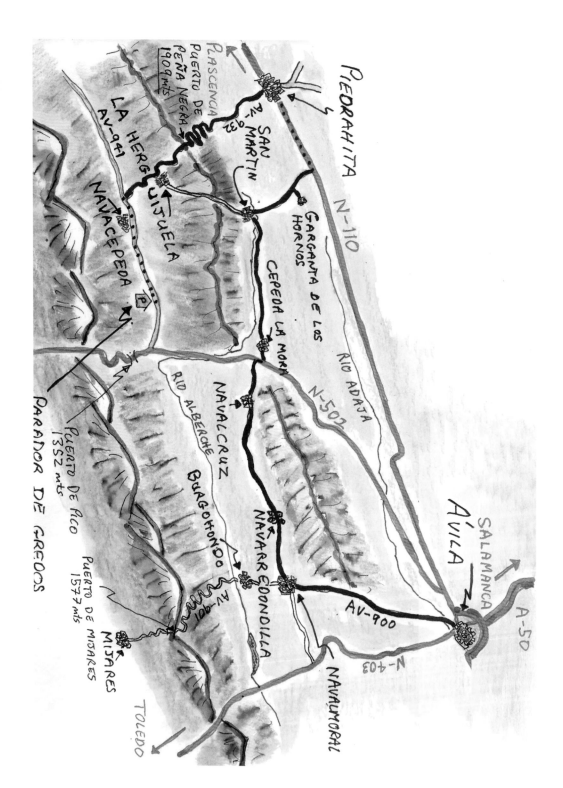

10 km after San Martin on the AV-510 I came to Cepeda la Mora, with a convenient *fuente* filling a big stone trough. I stopped to refill my water bottle from the *fuente* spout and was surprised to see half a dozen fish swimming around in the trough.

I crossed the N-502 and took to the AV-P-415. For a while, a continuation of the wide plain until the road turned down beside the Arroyo Chiquillo. Just before Navalacruz I found a lunch stop beside another *fuente*.

My journey continued to Ávila, it was fascinating, and instructive finding this slightly different route. One that took me right off the 'beaten track' and into an area that was removed from the tourist route. An area where life worked to the agriculture and the seasons - self-sufficient.

Another point for using real maps not satnavs or even just online maps; It is about being able to spot interesting features, twists and bends in the roads, or isolated towns and villages that will give you a unique experience as you travel through.

Onward to Salamanca...

Salamanca

2004 and I am blown into Salamanca by a bruising wind and go straight to the reasonable campsite at the Hotel Regio. You can catch a bus from the hotel car park to the city centre. A short walk through the back streets will bring you to the Plaza Mayor, a great place to sit in the sun, out of the wind with a glass of wine for company. Preferably a nice earthy Ribera de Duero. Salamanca is truly a city of golden stone. The Cathedral in its gothic splendour is a huge contrast to Moorish Córdoba.

A very busy city, a very 'international' one. You'll probably see more nationalities here than in Madrid. Its Universities and Colleges are world renowned and it is a major tourist attraction. The Plaza Mayor has to rank amongst the best in the World. It is a space you walk into and catch your breath, it is huge, it is beautiful. The sound is special, the tall buildings and small entrances cut all mechanical noise from the outer city, all you hear is footfalls and conversation, the rustle of clothing, the gay shouts of children, the clink of cup and glass at the many tables. Like Zamora, Salamanca is on the Ruta de la Plata and you will see many carved or cast scallop shells marking the pilgrims way. The Ruta was actually built by the Romans as

a commercial route for goods and armies, linking the port of Cadiz in the south with that of Gijón in the north. In fact it may well have continued up into France to connect with the roads to Rome. Later it became a route for the wealth of South America and for the pilgrims headed for Santiago de Compostela.

In 2014 when I did my Spanish course here I was delighted that the bar attached to the Don Quijote school had a Moto Guzzi on the wall! The course was good but my lack of comprehension of grammar was a severe handicap. However, the other students and being here for a whole week were great.

I found that crossing the river on the pedestrian Puente Romano just down from the cathedral, one could wander along to the left and find the Bar La Pachamama which is very popular with locals and in my view better and

cheaper than many places serving tourists in the main city. It is quite small but there are pleasant views across the river and one can just 'people watch' or sketch with a handy *vaso de vino*. When fed you can continue a short distance further and stagger back to the city across the Puente de Enrique Esteban. If you've got more than a day or so here you might like to get a guide book and make a list of what you want to get to, or if you are like me, just go and wander around and see what you find.

If like me you are a fan of Bernard Cornwell's Sharpe series then you might take Sharpe's Sword with you and visit Arapiles, the site of the Battle of Salamanca (22nd July 1812). Unlike the battlefield at Talavera (Sharpe's Eagle) this is pretty much as it was. If you are coming or going to Ávila then you could also stop in the pretty town of Alba de Tormes where, had the Spanish held or destroyed the bridge, the French army would have been caught by the English cavalry and probably totally defeated. Wellington it was said, was not amused. However Salamanca was a very successful battle and showed that Wellington could be a decisive and attacking General. He had about 5,000 causalities but the French lost around 14,000. He went on to enter Madrid in August and even reached Burgos before having to retreat to winter quarters at

Lesser Arapiles from Greater Arapiles with Salamanca in the distance.

Ciudad Rodrigo. It is interesting to visit Ciudad Rodrigo for as with Jaca and Almeida the fortifications are not built over and one can see the long sloping 'glacis' that was designed to absorb the impact of cannon balls and not allow them to hit at the base of the defensive walls. These castles are in stark contrast to the high vertical walls and towers of such as Ávila that were built before artillery was a serious concern.

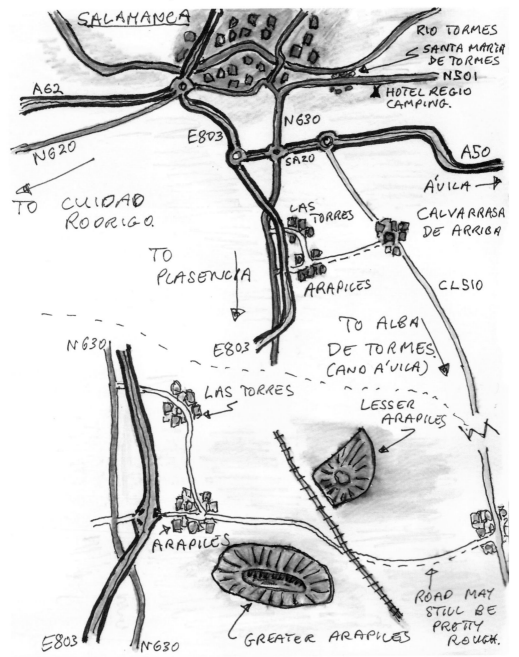

Zamora

Zamora is a pleasant city riding on a bluff above the Duero. Old castle walls still rim the heights above the bend in the river which provided it with its defensive prow. A poor sister perhaps to grand Salamanca, but the advantage being that it is far less touristy and does have a very

Figures from the Semana Santa

grand cathedral built between 1151 and 1174, which is one of the best examples of the Romanesque in Spain. The city's importance was always a lot to do with it being situated on the Via de la Plata.

Zamora is rightly famed for its Easter parades - Semana Santa, and you can see the amazing *pasos* - figures on floats, in the Museo de Semana Santa de Zamora. The city was important at many times in history as different kings took control. It was so often fought over that the Spanish have a saying; *"No se ganó Zamora en una hora"* - Zamora wasn't won in an hour. It claims to have more Romanesque churches than any other city in Europe.

The parador here is in the Palacio de los Condes de Alba y Aliste dating back to the 15th century and though it has been through a few 'modernisations' these are all very sympathetic. It is situated not far from the cathedral, high on the prow of the city. Sit out on the terrace at the end of the day with *un vaso de vino tinto* with that distinctive Duero granitic tang.

Watch the White Storks come grandly circling in to their huge nests which dot the buildings, they obviously appreciate Romanesque architecture. Mind you, they also like pylons. In Extremadura there are places where every pylon has two or three huge nests balanced on its structure. The Plaza Viriato at the front of the Parador has typical Spanish plane trees that are grafted together and in the summer provide a cool green canopy.

This city, like Burgos, is a great place to take time out from busyness, to sit or stroll the streets for a day. Don't give yourself a list of things you have to see, just see what comes along, what you get round to. There is always an *otra mañana*. Go to the castle walls and look out over the plains that stretch to distant hazy, blue mountains, or walk down by the Duero and stop at a small bar for some *tapas*.

In 2004 I met up for the first time with old friends of my father. Though they had some English it was as rusty as my Spanish. However, through the next three days of hospitality and discussion we all improved linguistically. The days passed in a wonderful meaty stew of mangled Spanish and English, architecture and restaurants, remembrance of my father and discussions of all manner of things.

It is perhaps appropriate to tell you how we've become such good friends. My father basically picked them up from a car park in Somerset. He noticed they were Spanish and introduced himself, ending up inviting them to my parents' house for lunch, in his way saying the *'me casa, su casa'* – 'my house, is your house', that I have been privileged to receive a few times in Spain. It was the link that meant we met and have done over the years since, always remembering my father and mother but developing our own deep friendship. Like my father, Manuel is always ready to sketch and always ready to get into convoluted conversation or jump up and say *"venga, vamos a...."* - 'let's go to...' One evening, we visited an amazing underground Bodega in nearby El Perdigón, a nondescript village where there is an area of criss-crossing sandy tracks, between them low mounds and odd little brick chimneys jutting from the ground. Here and there are what look like small brick sheds, each with a single door. Entering one of these you descend by a narrow stairway, deep into the ground. Perhaps

twelve or twenty metres down to converted wine *bodegas* which have a charcoal fire or *un horno* - oven, and a well-stocked bar. Great food and atmosphere, if you are not claustrophobic.

In 2016 I had another happy reunion with Manuel and Tensi. We'd had some texts between us but I wasn't sure whether they were in Madrid or Zamora. I was in the bar of the hotel in Toro and had just watched Wales' fantastic achievement in beating Belgium, to go through to an all-time high position in Euro 2016, it was about 9.30pm and I was considering turning in. The next moment Tensi was at my shoulder. The evening was spent going from one bar or restaurant to another in the company of Manuel, Tonio and Canto who has perhaps the clearest Spanish I have come across, which really helps my understanding and conversational attempts. A fact that is also useful is that as the Spanish love to talk and discuss things, they rarely give up on finding a way to make you understand what they are on about. Tapas and wine flowed and we had a great evening with me finally getting to bed after 1am.

In 2004 when I left Zamora for Burgos I had spotted on the map a *mirador* - look-out, at Autilla del Pino, close to Palencia (don't confuse it with Plasencia) and it was well worth the visit. For me this Mirador de la Tierra de Campos - 'Lookout of the Land of Fields', encompasses so much of the

Mirador de la Tierra de Campos. *Cerca* - near to Palencia

visual joy of Spain, here in a nondescript, hot and dusty plain, a small hill can make all the difference, the sky is so huge, the plains of Castilla y Leon take on their real grandeur. Perhaps in the hazy far distance a faint dark line divides the dusty yellow from the blue sky and hints at the heights of the Picos de Europa and Cantabrian mountains. Just breathe in the distance.

The Tierra de Campos stretches across the provinces of León, Zamora, Valladolid and Palencia. A landscape ironed out by man since Roman and Visigothic times at least. There are more bustards (large European emu's that can fly) here than probably anywhere else in the world, catching sight of them is another thing, unless they are flying when their shape distinguishes them from the odd Griffon Vulture venturing over the plains. A male Great Bustard has a wingspan of up to two and a half metres, similar size to the vulture but narrower wings and trailing legs. You will however, see many larks and pippits. The common Crested Lark is easy to identify at a glance but for the rest you will need to stop. It can be worth it though to identify a Thekla or a Calandra!

I have enjoyed a number of roads across the Tierra, from Zamora the CL-612, from Toro the ZA-705 and over the years most of the little white ones in between. Skirting Palencia I have gone north to Carrión de los Condes on the CL-615 and then picked up the old N-120 (Camino de Santiago) avoiding as much as possible the new *autopista* A-231 that has supplanted it on the way east to Burgos.

That 2004 round trip was of around 3,000 miles in just over ten days. The memories and experience mirroring the trip, some events seem to have sped by, flashes of encapsulated moments, flown free of the blurring passage of miles. Others are there to savour, long and sensual.

2016 was about the same distance and covered some of the same ground. 12 years on it was just as enthralling and vibrant an experience. My Spanish is a bit better, I have refined the way I interact with those I meet. Hopefully am more open and accepting, more ready to do it their way, and am more aware of what that way might be.

There were bad moments; being eaten alive in that crummy Tabernas Hotel, blown sideways by unrelenting wind, frustration at my inability to communicate better in Spanish. But these are the salt and pepper, the darkness and pain that allow the light of my adventures to blaze out in my memory.

<u>Toro</u>

Toro is one of those little towns that are easy to pass by. Lying between Zamora and Tordesillas it can be fitted into a route to or from Salamanca. The A-11 by-passes it but the old N-122 goes pretty much through it.

It is again a place of enormous history, the Romans called it Albucella and in 1369 Enrique II summoned his first Cortes (parliament) here. Juan II of Castilla was born here in 1404. On one of the roundabouts there is a huge stone block, that with study and imagination turns into the *toro*, bull of Toro an ancient Celtiberian totem. It is also a centre for Mudéjar art and wine. During the Peninsular war against Napoleon, Sir John Moore started the terrible winter retreat to A Coruña from here, and later Wellington amassed an army of 100,000 here for the final push that expelled the French from Iberia.

To find the beauty of Toro, follow signs for the Hotel Juan II (they appear closer to the town centre), this will bring you, via back streets, around the pedestrian central street and Plaza Mayor. You will pass the remains of the Alcázar and there is plenty of parking in a broad open area here, or you can go on and park outside the hotel (as long as there are spaces, it doesn't have a large parking area). To the right of the hotel reception, are steps leading down to a bar and restaurant which is very good, and has a great terrace that looks out over the Duero River to far hills. In front of the

hotel is a pleasant little park and the main 12th century church of Santa Maria la Mayor which is impressive. Worth a look inside for the painting La Virgen de la Mosca (the Virgin of the Fly) which unusually shows the Virgin pregnant. Walk to the edge of the park and enjoy a great view down the steep bluff Toro sits on, to the old bridge that crosses the Duero. This is number three of the great rivers of Spain at 895 km, in Portugal it becomes the Douro. Along its length there are great wine growing areas, the soil and waters give a distinctive taste to the wines produced. Toro wine is fabulous. There are some great local *bodegas* and shops where you can get a really good deal on some exquisite *vino*. Walk round the corner past the church and you will find the main shopping area, it is reminiscent of Chester with half-timbered medieval buildings leading up to the Torre del Reloj, its gateway to the outer town. It has a lovely atmosphere.

I have stayed in the hotel a number of times and can really recommend it. Ask for a balcony room and enjoy sitting out with a cold beer as the evening washes the river and hills with a more subtle light than the strong, hard, midday sun. As the noises of the day wind down, you can hear the screaming of the endlessly circling swifts and perhaps the rush of the weir below the bridge, where a lone fisherman stands in the streaming water casting into the turbulence. If you are on one or two *motos*, ask if you can put them in the courtyard outside reception for the night and I expect they will say yes, as they did with me.

As always in Spanish towns and villages, it is possible you will arrive when there is a fiesta. Toro has an active musical and theatre life and a nice little theatre (Teatro Latorre). I once saw some excellent Flamenco dancers there.

2007. Hotel Juan Dos at Toro. At 10pm in the main street there are all sorts of things happening. A stage is being built and up the street either a bridesmaids' group or a hen party are wearing antenna and on the rampage; singing, whistling and chanting, I know not what. Further up towards the towered gateway a traditionally dressed group, in hose and fancy leather slippers are playing guitars and maracas. Amongst all this human noise the swifts scream in squadrons round the roofs and eaves. A lone White Stork - *siguena* gracefully flaps once and glides in at rooftop height, it clatters its bill as it lands on its nest above the busy roadies setting up lighting stands. Grandparents keep an eye on little kids as they run around amongst the crowd. Do the *siguena* chicks grow up with a need for noise and song late into the night? They watch from above as the sky fades to a deep azure, their parents coming in from the fields and the river, as the last light fades above and the lights below take over.

In the park by the church high above the Duero the last swifts cry out as they head to roost. Down the bluff by the river the crickets' evening song competes with the muted roar of the weir. I return to the street where the disco is just starting up, though it is almost drowned out by human voices. Of course the little kids are the first to start dancing to the beat, still watched by their grandparents, or some one's grandparents. Later I stand on my balcony, the music and dancing just audible from the town. Below, the river gleams and above is a vast, bright star field. The sound of the weir soothes my sleep.

Sanabria

If one uses the N-103 between Braga and Bragança to come or go from northern Portugal then it is not much of a detour to take in Sanabria, which is north-east of Bragança. This is a town and a region somewhat off the normal foreign tourist routes but well used by the Spanish. It is about two hours from Zamora and four from Madrid. The region is studded with lakes and *embalses* that use the Rio Tera. Sanabria Lake - Lago de Sanabria, is the biggest natural lake (glacial) in the whole of Spain. With wooded areas and many campsites close to the lakes it has numerous water sports facilities, and the beaches are sandy.

The town of Puebla de Sanabria goes back to at least the 10th century. It sits quite impressively on a bluff above the river.

The modern town was built around the castle of the Count of Benavente dating from the 15th century.   There is the church of Nuestra Señora de Azogue from the 13th century and the Hermitage of San Cayetano, from the 17th century.   The central streets are great to wander around.

The Sierra de la Culebra nearby has quite a few wolf packs. There are excellent walking trails in the Lake Sanabria National Park.

The mountains of northern Portugal on the N-103

Hang A Right

That is; go right from Santander or Bilbao. The Costa Verde - Green Spain, wonder why it is called that? Could just be because it gets rather more rain than the rest of Spain, yes it rains on the plain, but only after it has been raining on the Costa Verde! Still it is a beautiful land, a lot like my homeland *Cymru* - Wales. Close to Santander there are many fishing villages to explore. Many are well promoted for tourists, but still fun to visit. Santillana del Mar, San Vicente del Barquera and Comillas are just three of the best known. If you go to Comillas take a look at Gaudí's 'El Caprico' it may well tempt you to visit Barcelona one day.

Just outside Santander to the north-east is the Peña Cabarga Parque de Carbárceno, where there is an unusual and impressive zoo, 750 hectares of former open-pit mines. There are around a hundred different animals from five continents living in the large pits, enclosed by natural cliffs for

the most part, often with more than one species together. It feels about as natural and as good as a zoo can get. One can get remarkably close to the animals without peering through chain-link fencing. We visited on a family trip and the kids really enjoyed it.

The Museum of the Inquisition in Santillana del Mar was not quite so successful. I think my wife and I had visions of something like a Monty Python sketch. It was in fact terribly real with all sorts of torture instruments matter of factly explained. We were horrified, particularly as one of the three kids was a niece. The kids were un-phased and we had trouble trying to

hurry them round and out, before in our minds they got too much material for nightmares. Ice creams to the rescue.

A couple of years ago I found a nice campsite about halfway from Bilbao to Santander, at Islares between Castro-Urdiales and Laredo. I had checked out a campsite, I think in Laredo but it was inland and didn't look great, then I went to the tourist information in Castro-Urdiales which was situated close to the lovely and picturesque harbour. I ended up going back toward Santander and Islares. Pleasant people, little shop and bar with a restaurant a short walk away and close to a sandy beach. The run in to the Bilbao ferry in the morning was quick and easy.

June 2015. I am on a new *Viaje de España*. Knowing roughly where I wanted to go I first checked www.paradores.es for any good deals that fitted in. I got a good one at Villafranca del Bierzo which was a reasonable 400 km or so after coming off the ferry at Santander, and in the right direction for visiting with friends near Arcos de Valdevez in northern Portugal the following day. I have enjoyed passing along this coast a few times, with excursions up into the Picos. The Picos de Europa - The Peaks of Europe; they are not really the highest and largest range, but give them a bit of credit for being pretty spectacular, partly because they stand so close to the sea which gives a real sense of scale.

The *Autopista* A-8 runs west along the whole coast past Gijón and all the way to A Coruña. Certainly, coming out of Santander this is the road to grab, but once past Torrelavega I look to get off it onto the N-634 which the A-8 replaced. It just makes the 'going' so much more fun and means you go through places like San Vicente de la Barquera. The road is closer to the wonderful beaches and rocky coves and it's easy to stop if you feel like it. Just before Llanes (worth a stop) the A-8 has been built on top of the 'N' road and you have to do a section of motorway or transfer to the AS-263 which you can follow through Llanes and on along the coast, diving under the A-8 periodically on its way to Ribadesella which is a pretty town with boats and golden beaches and the impressive backdrop of the Picos unless of course they've hidden themselves in cloud. Here you can pick up the N-632 to continue westward.

It can be a bit more of a navigating challenge to travel 'off-*autovia*' as your SatNav will probably spend its time trying to put you back on the motorway and the road signs will only mention local places, not telling you that this is a viable alternative route to Gijón. But with a map and keeping the sea to your right, the rewards are great.

Picos de Europa

A lot of people visit Potes and Fuente De which are the 'big deal' of the Picos and worth doing. However depending on time of year they are very touristy and filled with RV's and coaches. If heading that way, then you grab the N-621 at San Vicente de la Barquera and will soon be threading some spectacular scenery. At Fuente De in the heart of the Picos there is a Parador and a cable car up to the peaks above which can get very, very busy in the season (be there for 9am) but the views from the Mirador at the top are stupendous (on a clear day!)

In 2011 I was cutting back towards Burgos from near Villaviciosa and was told a great route to take through the Picos. On the N-632 just east of Colunga there is a roundabout and you can set off south on the AS-260, you can also get on to this from the A-8 junction close to Coceña. A lot of local bikers go up here on the weekends because a few kilometres up this fantastic road you have the Mirado del Fitu which has incredible views

The Picos de Europa

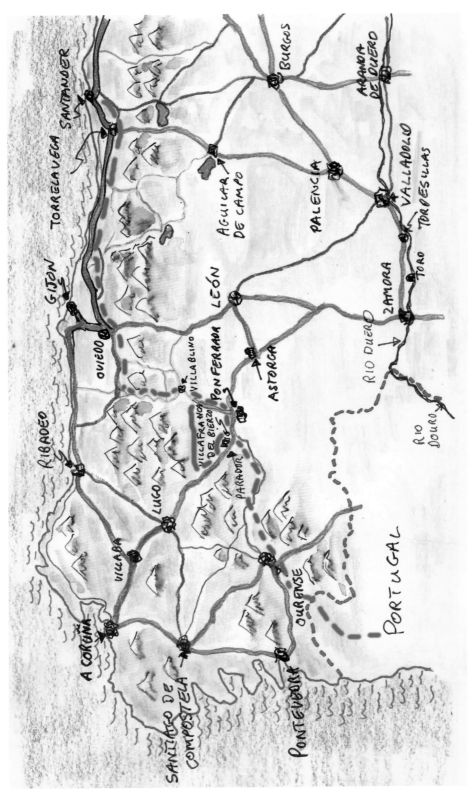

of the coast and mountains (and a bar). I have not seen the views myself; the day I was there the cloud level was a few hundred metres below it - drat, have to go back. The road beyond to Coviella was pretty good. Oh, by the way, do watch for large horned beasties in the road. And if on a bike, the just as dangerous waste products. At Coviella take the N-625 for Cangas de Onis and Riaño. Personally, this road is one of those ones you want to travel again and again. The road has quite a job threading its way through these massive mountains, trying to find elbow room with rushing rivers at the bottom of *canóns* that are so deep it is a job to crane your head back far enough to see the sliver of blue sky far above. There are hundreds of adventures waiting for you in the Picos. For me, a flexible approach to the itinerary is by far the best. Don't nail yourself to a week of Picos and then it happens to rain all week. If it is raining anywhere along the Cantabrian and Picos mountains it is very often dry south on the *meseta* in Castille y Leon. So change plans, there will be other wonderful things waiting for you.

In 2010 the good old 'Parador Amigos' gave me a great deal at the Parador de Cervera de Pisuerga. This is between Riaño and Aguilar de Campoó. Aguilar is on the A-67, the main motorway from Santander to Valladolid and southern Portugal. It was my first day in Spain and it was a brilliant one. You could whip down the A-67 from Santander and be there in a little over an hour. Or, you could spend all day doing it, see Potes, lace the Picos and arrive sated with vistas. The parador is a modern one but as always, has great, comfortable rooms. My balcony had a tremendous view and nesting Alpine Swifts right above my head under the eaves.

After that little detour into the Picos let's get back on track for the Parador at Villafranca del Bierzo. At Ribadesella, I left the coast and enjoyed the N-634 for Oviedo. Of course road signage will try and send you there on the A-64, resist. When you get to Oviedo it gets a little complicated.

Like other cities in Spain you have the original outer ring roads, then the early 'N' road bypass and now the *autopista* further out again. I got a bit muddled with the A-66 and 63, the O-11 and 12 and the N-630. I stopped to look at the map and tried to work out where I was in relation to the N-634 that I had lost. A young man stopped his car and enquired (in Spanish) if I needed help, I told him where I was headed and he told me to follow him. He led me round and about through the underpasses and slip roads and waved me cheerily onto the right road. There were three other times on the trip when people volunteered to help or direct me.

The N-634 has been superseded by the A-63 which you could use instead. In 2015 it ground to a halt in a roundabout near Doriga but by now probably goes over the Rio Narcea and past the next big town of Cornellana. Whether on the 'N' or the 'A' road you want to get onto the AS-15 before you cross the river to head up through the Cantabrians. The AS-15, and then AS-227 took me through some great passes to find Villablino. An even more exciting route looks to be possible by turning off the N-634/A-63 earlier at Udrion and finding the AS-228 which leads to the Desifiladero del Teverga. *desifiladero's* are always a good bet.

Villafranca del Bierzo

From Villablino it is an easy run down to Ponferrada which is only about 20 km from Villafranca del Bierzo and another modern parador which is excellent value. I actually took an involuntary tour of the town as I missed the entrance to the parador which is very close as you come off the N-VI. Around 400 kms for the day, quite tiring but what a lot of country and some treasured moments like watching a Red-backed Shrike which brought back memories of the rare nesting of them close to my Suffolk home in the 1970's. I walked into town the next morning hunting for socks. Somehow all the careful packing and preparation had lost all my socks. This was good for me; second day in Spain and my Spanish was *basura* - rubbish, so going into various shops in search of socks made me meet people, communicate and feel again the propensity for helpfulness of the Spanish people. I got some good ones eventually, in a hardware store.

Spain is divided up into Comunidades Autónomas, Extremadura and Andalucía for example. Within these are provinces which all have their own character and often a slightly or wholly in the case of Pais Vasco - Basque country, different language. The character of the land and its history has a lot to do with these differences of which the people are rightly proud.

I started in Cantabria and then came Asturias. Asturias was traditionally the milk producer for the whole of Spain, unfortunately that fell foul of EU Common Agriculture policy and today the dominant agriculture seems to be eucalyptus which has replaced the small farms. The next most important thing here is cider - *sidra*. There are many bars dedicated to it called *sidrerias*. It is poured in a very special way - *escanciar*, the pourer, holding the glass as low as possible and the bottle as high as possible overhead. The pour is accomplished whilst looking anywhere but at the glass which is not filled, as you are supposed to knock it back straight away to get the full flavour.

Now in Villafranca, I was in Galicia, the western most part of Spain, with a Visigothic and Celtic heritage and its own language of Gallego. You notice the difference on the road signs. It is a good preparation in that respect for Portugal. The wine of D.O. Bierzo is coming into its own these days, so of course I did some sampling. If you like octopus then *Pulpo Gallego* is the way to have it.

The fast route for the next day would be under 300 km and take about three and a half hours. My route took nearer 8 hours and well over 300 km, partly because somewhere I had seen impressive pictures of the Canón do Sil. As I would be passing it before Ourense, it seemed like a good idea to investigate, in addition I would have to pass through the *pueblo* of Sober,

which was irresistible. The conjunction with D.O.A de... very applicable to riding a motorbike.

I turned off the N-120 at Canaval onto the LU-P-5901, this was real backroads stuff, small road and small villages. Eventually on a rough forestry road, I got to the Miradoiro de O Boqueiriño and the Canón. Unfortunately it was very misty, though the cloud shifted at times to give me tantalising glimpses of the spectacular gorge and river below. I decided to make the most of it, having a snack and birdwatching. Then the quietness and the peacefulness, the soft caressing light and moisture dewed trees began to grow on me. The odd breath of wind stirred the pine needles into a sigh and brought me their scent, and the subtle-voiced Woodlark I had been trying to identify at last gave me a decent view. I find these moments of peace very much a part of the whole therapeutic effect of my journeys through Iberia.

After passing Ourense I wanted to get onto the southern side of the Rio Miño which the Rio Sil had joined. I finally managed this at Ribadavia where I got off the N-120 and onto either the OU-0305 or OU-403; the main thing was getting onto the OU-402 for Cortegada and Pont Barxas on the Portugese border where it became the N-301 briefly and then the N-202 and N-304. One of those bits of country where remembering the next few towns is the safest bet. This route follows the river Miño to Monção where I turned south on the N-101 for Arcos de Valdevez.

Portugese looks like Spanish but sounds like Polish, full of 'shh' and 'chh', Arcos becoming 'Arcoshhh'. Many Portugese understand Spanish, though they may not like their big neighbours very much, who historically have tried to conquer them from time to time. Apart from their hardy resistance, the very rough mountains that the invaders had to cross helped to keep them independent. The French invasion during the Peninsular War found that out. Incidentally, Portugal is Great Britain's oldest Treaty Ally. Our close ties cemented by the long work of the Port Barons like Osborne, Taylor, Dow and Cockburn who settled down in Porto a long time before the Algarve happened.

I spent a wonderful couple of days with my English friend and his Portugese wife. Lots of lovely food, wine, discussion of the world, and of the last 40 years since we had been under the same roof. We walked up in the hills above his little village into a wonderful forested and rocky area. He has frequently been able to see wolves up here and works to try and build trust between locals and the wolves. They are not protected here, in the way they are not far away in the Paisagem Protegida do Corno de Bico. We didn't see any wolves but saw a few Bonelli's Eagles, Cirl Bunting and Black Kites and some wolf tracks in a muddy place which was for me, very exciting.

The time came to move on as I had booked the Hotel Fortaleza de Almeida in advance. This wasn't really an easy day's travel because it was over 350 km, my planned route was going to be fairly back-road, and I didn't manage to leave until 2pm, after a lovely lunch. BUT, it was a challenge, it did push my 'edge', and at the day's end, when at 8.30 I put the bike on its side-stand outside the hotel, it was worth the adventure.

It was that day I really started noticing the difference between the road systems of Spain and Portugal. Portugal is a much poorer country which is obvious in the small rural villages and in the state of the back roads. Spain is similar in a way to the UK; rural roads, 'A' (N) roads, which have then been superseded by motorways and in Spain quite a few toll motorways. Portugal seems to have only motorways, mostly tolled and rural roads which are often quite rough. On the back roads one is soon aware that Portugal is a much smaller country and generally more densely settled. So one is far more frequently having to reduce speed and negotiate villages.

That day I adapted my route planning for Portugal, still doing wiggly back roads where they looked good and would make sense, and using motorways to gain time and distance in between. In Spain one can make average speeds on the 'N' roads not that much less than on the *autopista* or *autovia*, in Portugal it is a lot slower 'off-*pista*'. By the way if you like curves in your roads then the N-103 from Bragança to Braga has 200 km of them!

My friend had suggested a detour to Montalegre about 10 km north of the Rio Rabagão lake on the N-103 which he said was well worth visiting, and had a Roman history. Unfortunately I was already beginning to worry about time by that point and so passed it by. And by the time I got to Chaves I had decided to abandon the next section of planned back roads which would have seen me continue towards Bragança before turning south for Mirandela. If you look at big road map of Portugal you will see that there are a lot of east to west motorways; these are following all those river valleys down to the sea. Crossing between them gives you much more varied scenery but rougher roads. Well, I zipped down the motorway till past Villa Real and when I hit the Douro, I took the N-222 eastward to get me over towards the Spanish border and Almeida. This was an enjoyable stretch with great views of the Douro valley and lots of bends to loosen me up after the motorway. The N-222 became the N-332 and brought me to Castelo Rodrigo which I would have explored if not for the time getting on. All down the border-lands are castles and their remains. Their designs and ages vary greatly, from those that stood against the Moors to those designed to defeat the French. Castelo Rodrigo castle stands out from a distance, high and vertical. Just over 20 kms south is the very contrasting castle of Almeida. On the long, long straight road I kept expecting to pick

out the famous castle but it was not until I was within a kilometre that I could begin to pick out fortifications. This is a truly amazing town to visit and the Hotel Fortaleza de Almeida is a great place to stay. To my delight, a Hoopoe greeted my arrival.

Almeida

Don't get the Portugese Almeida mixed up with the Spanish one which is about 100 km away north of Ledesma. One year I took it in having seen a road sign and of course it wasn't THE Almeida.

I am very glad that I have a policy of not doing a huge amount of advance research on places I go to, there is so much detail now on Google Earth that one might almost as well not bother actually going. There is only one way to experience Almeida, go there. As you get close to the walls they become more sinister, not imposing perhaps, but they would be no joke to climb if defended. Passing through the tunnel into the castle is a memorable experience. I followed the road close to the outer walls up to the hotel, the extent of the place becoming more and more apparent. You cannot appreciate this place with out walking its walls and letting the history seep

into you. What a history; in 1641 with renewed Portuguese independence it was decided to modernise the fortress, the method of design based on those in Antoine de Ville's book (1628) - 'Les Fortifications'. This had become the standard work for 'modern' fortresses that could withstand the increasing might of artillery on the battlefield. It is hexagonal with six massive bulwarks (instead of traditional walls) with watch towers and six associated ravelins below. A moat was added defence and apparently where all the waste water from the fortress went. There were over 100 guns, forty or more 18 pounders or larger.

In the Peninsular War in August 1810 the French army laid siege to Almeida, which was commanded by the British Army Brigadier-General William Cox. He was pretty confident he could hold up the French advance for a long time as he was well provisioned, had lots of gunpowder, 4,000 Portugese troops and some British regulars. The gunpowder and ammunition was stored in the old medieval castle basements. Unfortunately on the first day of French bombardment a shell ignited a trail of gunpowder presumably from a leaking keg that had been taken from the magazine to the defending guns. The magazine exploded with what has been said to be one of the biggest pre-nuclear explosions. Over 600 defenders were killed outright, the castle was completely blown away and the top of the town flattened. Cox surrendered the next day. Bernard Cornwell has used this event in his book Sharpe's Gold.

In my room, after raiding the mini-bar (really shouldn't have as it always costs, but I'd had a long ride...), I enjoyed a *paseo* around the walls,

Wheatear and Water Pippits flitting from battlement to battlement. The map of the fortress is impressive, but is nothing compared to actually walking around it. It is not a big town and maybe in the height of the season it could become very busy. I was there at the end of June (pre-season) and it was delightfully quiet, with very few other tourists.

The next day, a fresh and sunny morning, I walked around the town and sat outside a pleasant bar with my breakfast, *café solo* and a croissant. Receiving nods from locals popping in, I watched the aerial skills of the House Martins flying in to their nests under the opposite eaves.

One of the reasons I wanted to visit Almeida was because of an idea for a guided tour visiting Peninsular War battlefields, particularly the ones that Bernard Cornwell has had Sharpe at. It would be the theme of the trip, the rest of the experience being about great back roads, great food and great scenery. The Five Eagles Tour I organised was a very successful tour; the theme being the five different species of eagle that one can see in Spain, all in a week.

The next place on this journey was close to the Lines of Torres Vedras, one of the biggest, and most successful military defence systems ever constructed. It was instigated by Arthur Wellesley - Duke of Wellington in 1810, to defeat the third attempt by Napoleon to conquer the whole of Iberia and eject the British. Some friends from the UK were flying into Lisbon and so we had arranged to meet up at Arruda dos Vinhos close to a section of The Lines, around 400 km from Almeida.

Soon it was time to be on the road again. I was fairly successful with my back roads for the first 140 km till Castelo Branco. N-340, 324 to Sabugal and N-233 to Penamacor. Not bad roads and some birdwatching; Booted Eagles, Griffon Vulture, Little Egret and some vibrant Bee-eaters. I found that there are a lot of very small villages not marked on the map, nearly all with their radar controlled lights; it is interesting, but does mean that it takes longer than expected to get from 'A' to 'B'.

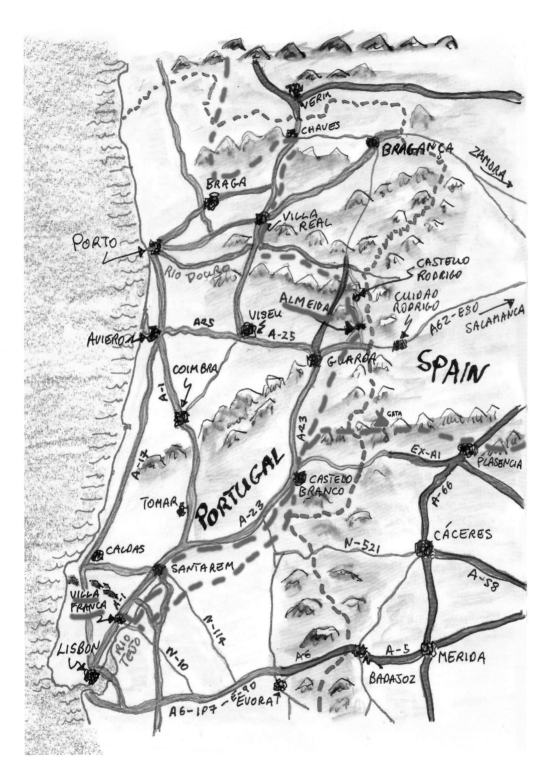

As I headed further south the temperature was heading up towards 40°. Luckily I like heat, though I do make a point of putting sunscreen on my face (open-face helmet) and of drinking water whenever I stop to look at the map or a bird. The dry, hot air will dehydrate you quite quickly and you don't realise how much you sweat (till you get in a room with yourself at the end of the day). My intention had been to skirt Castelo Branco to the south on small roads and continue back-roading. Time and inclination got the better of me and I decided to do some motorway and notch up some distance, I therefore got onto what seems to be called the A23 IP-2 E-802 (See the 'Really Useful Stuff' section at the rear of the book for details of the Via Verde transponder and other ways of paying tolls on the Portugese *autopista*). I cruised past Castelo Branco and carried on all the way to Torres Novas - 120 km of not much to do for an hour or so. The N-118 that I swung onto was a better more involving road skirting the edge of the Rio Tagus flood plain. Of course, back to radar controlled lights...

The N-10 took me over the wide Tagus on the Ponte Marechal Carmona and bang into Vila Franca de Xira. Portugese road signage it has to be said, is rather hit and miss, it can all be hits, bang on and then suddenly all misses with whole towns disappearing. The A-1 E-80 shoots right over the top of the town but I needed a local road to get to Arruda which is about 14 km away. Signs for schools etc. etc. but not for local destinations. This required trying my Spanish on some Portugese office workers, a very nice lady replied in English and though she sent me on a route that was over 20 km, it did not involve diving through the back streets of the town looking for the elusive N-248 but took me on clear roads via Carregado.

Arriving in Arruda I had some difficulty finding the Hotel Quinta de Santa Maria. Eventually two very nice young ladies led me with their car to its gates.

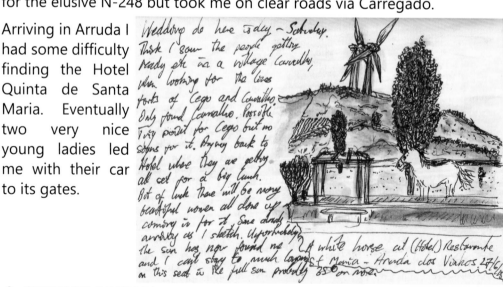

Arruda dos Vinhos

I had booked into Hotel Quinta de Santa Maria on the N-248 just out of the town. It is to some extent a restaurant with rooms as there are only six in the main manor house, they are nice and in June reasonably priced. There are also four apartments so a family could be very comfortable. As well as its high quality restaurant it has a big garden and swimming pool. The octopus dish I had was delicious, with potatoes and spinach and good sized portions. I was able to walk into town from the hotel though the first road section had no pavement.

I expect there are many other options for a place to stay close to the Lines. I was very happy with my choice. The town being somewhat tucked away is pleasant. As you might guess from the name, the wine industry has been very important in its history and continues to be.

The Lines of Torres Vedras are a network of 152 fortifications that though not continuous were designed to cover each other so as to be very hard to attack. Constructed on the hilly terrain between the Atlantic and the river Tagus they defended the Lisbon peninsular. With the supremacy of the Royal Navy at sea and in the Tagus estuary it was the only way the French could hope to attack Lisbon, take Portugal and expel the British.

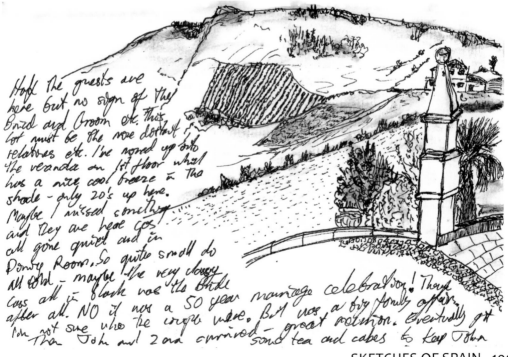

Half the guests are here but no sign of the Bride and Groom etc. This lot must be the more distant relatives etc. I've moved up onto the veranda on 1st floor which has a nice cool breeze in the shade - only 20's up here. Maybe I missed something and they are here cos all gone quiet and in Dining Room. So quite small do all told - maybe the very dowdy lass all in black was the Bride after all. NO it was a 50 year marriage celebration! They were a big family affair. I'm not sure who the couple were. But was a great occasion. Eventually got the John and 2nd arrived - some tea and cakes to keep John.

The idea for the Lines had been around since 1808 but it was not till after an inspection by Wellington in 1809 that work began. Amazingly, despite French spies in Lisbon, the huge undertaking was kept a secret for a year and was a total surprise to Marshall Masséna when he arrived before them.

At least 7,000 Portugese labourers (paid) had toiled to move mountains of earth and build the forts. In a way they were too strong because the French only made a couple of half-hearted attacks and Wellington could have done with a successful battle that would have reduced the French Army and with their long supply lines given them a difficult retreat.

I knew there were two forts close by and there was a signpost to them in the town. I followed this out up a small winding road towards the hills, passing through the village of Mata. Soon after, I spotted in passing a sign that said Ruta Forte dos Militares and an arrow pointing up a poorly surfaced side road. Oh well, turn round and up we go. We passed a house and the road immediately became a track. Luckily my Moto Guzzi Stelvio is not too easily scared and on we went, it was interesting/fun and we eventually came out back on the N-115-4, which is when I realised it was meant as a shortcut for walkers. DOH! I continued to the top of the ridge on the proper road, and found more brown signs for both Fort Cego and Carvalha, to the right. Carvalha was visible and easy to ride to, so up I went.

The views were great and having read up about the forts I could see the strategic value and how it would intersect with adjacent forts. I thought I could see Cego with my trusty binoculars to the west. Not really a lot to see otherwise, mounds and ditches and empty gun emplacements. From the brochures, books and flyers it was evident that quite a lot of EU money had been used to do excavations, improve access, put up road signs and promote the Lines as a tourist attraction. However, in the intervening years, upkeep appears to have been minimal.

I didn't find Fort Cego that day, though a concerted effort of map reading with my friend found it the next. The track to it passed very close to some industrial units and I suspect the signs for it had been deliberately destroyed.   Other sites which we tried to find further along the Lines towards Bucelas had obviously also lost their brown 'heritage' direction signs. The Lines of Torres Vedras Heritage and Visitors Centre in Bucelas is housed in the Museo do Vinho which takes up the major part. It was still well worth visiting and across the way was a superb wine shop. It may be that the visitor centres around Torres Vedras are different, but for me it was important to have recced at least part of the Lines and discovered what difficulties might arise before ever bringing a tour here.

Another sideline for Arruda is witches, the most famous being called the Witch Arruda, though it seems likely this was a name handed down amongst a group of healers possibly all from the same family. People travelled from great distances to see them.

After our car excursion to the Lines we had a very nice lunch of *Sopa del Dia* at the hotel before parting company around 2pm.

Portugal was hotting up, 40° plus, but I was on my way to cooler lands. Back into Spain. I found a pretty good back road route, having crossed the Tagus again at Villa Franca on the N-10, the second major road junction and the Infantado Restaurante roundabout I came to gave me the N-119 heading towards Coruche though not crossing the Rio Sorraia, to it but going on to Mora via a bit of N-251. Lots of long, long straights, good road and not too many villages. At Mora I turned north on the N-2 as far as Ponte de Sor. The road cruising beside the Albufeira da Barragem de Montargil, a big reservoir, for quite a distance. There were many places where one could get down to the water's edge.

From Ponte it was the N-244 and 118. I had tasted a fantastic cheese at Arruda that came from Nisa so it got on the route. I again used the A-23 to bypass Castelo Branco and reversed my journey to Penamacor.

The R-346 or N-569 now took me back into Spain and to Valverde del Fresno by which time it was called the EX-205. The terrain had been steadily becoming hillier since Penamacor, with bigger and bigger mountains looming ahead. The EX-305 and then down to the CC-6.1, brought me to the pleasant campsite at Gata.

Mañana I was heading for the high passes of the Sierra de Gredos and Sierra de Guadarrama.

Guadalupe

I came to Guadalupe from Herrara del Duque in 2016. It was an interesting ride, at first through fairly flat and rather barren lands and crossing the Embalse de Garcia de Sola where the blue waters reflected back the growing day's heat. I turned off the N-502 near Castilblanco on to the EX-316 for 28 km before getting onto the EX-116 for Puerto Llano, the roads getting smaller but at last the mountain peaks ahead getting bigger. The EX-102 then took me through more sparse but higher lands to a slightly confusing roundabout sign that said Guadalupe south to the left and Guadalupe north and Navalmoral straight on. I couldn't be bothered to stop and look at the map, so after going round the roundabout twice, for thinking time, I plumped for south. It turned out a nice approach through the riverine valley of the Rio Gaudalupejo which then opened up to reveal the towers of Guadalupe on a small hill below higher mountainsides.

The statue of the virgin is carved from cedar wood and is under a metre in height. It was supposed to have been buried here in AD 712 by monks

fleeing Sevilla in the face of the Moorish invasion. Luckily at the beginning of the 14th century, a shepherd boy saw a vision that led to the statue being rediscovered. Guadalupe never looked back, as a monastery and shrine, royal patronage and pilgrims promoted the development of the town.

Monfragüe

From Guadalupe to Monfragüe you are following an extraordinary concertina of hill ranges, look at the terrain map on Google and you will see what I mean. They run in a gentle curve for about 150 km from Herrara to south of Plasencia. EX-118 took me through pleasant wooded lands, sweeping bends and a mountain ridge to either side. At Castañar de Ibor I

turned onto the EX-386. A parade of subtly changing vistas, scrubby mountainside, rocky escarpments, olive groves and wooded areas as I threaded through the Sierra de Viejas. I dived under the A-5 and used a short piece of the N-V to Jaraicejo before heading up the EX-385 and EX-208 to Monfragüe. It was pretty hot in the little car park below the Castillo de Monfragüe but after climbing the steep steps to the castle I found a welcome breeze.

The view from the top is spectacular as the *castillo* is on the end of one of the long ridges. There were lots of Black Kites and Griffon Vultures, the former swooping around the tower, the latter lazily circling or heading for their cliff side nests in long slow glides. A weird algal bloom had turned much of the Embalse de José María de Oriol-Alcántara II a virulent green.

The Moors came here in AD 713 and built a defensive position on the remains of Celt and Roman structures. They called it *Al-Mofrag* meaning 'the abyss'. After the *reconquista*, the Christians added and developed it further and in the 12th century the Knights of the Order Monte Gaudio brought a Byzantine carved figure from the gates of Jerusalem to become the Virgin of Monfragüe, which is housed in the small chapel next to the main remaining castle tower.

The castle watches over the Parque Nacional de Monfragüe which covers over 18,000 hectares of lakes and forests. As well as the ubiquitous Griffon Vultures and Black Kites it is home to Black (Cinereous) Vultures, Imperial Eagles and some rare Black-shouldered Kites.

As a large party of school kids arrived, I left the castle and after a pleasant conversation with a German couple in the car park continued on through the cleft through which the *embalse* continues on to the Rio Tajo. Below the

castle where the road crosses the bridge there is a lakeside parking area, *fuente* and picnic tables. I stopped to watch a flock of Black Kites diving and swooping over the water. The first time I had seen them fishing. There was a Park Warden there, and for something to say I asked him whether the Black Kites were fishing. He said they were, and I then mentioned that it would be nice to see a Black Vulture. He thereupon went and got a

monocular telescope on a tripod from his van and set it up pointed at the opposite hillside. He told me to look and there on a massive pile of sticks in the top of a tree, were two Black Vultures. One was an adult and the other the chick, he told me. It was one of those cases where a little Spanish went a long way. We both knew the subject we were talking about and so despite my fairly poor vocabulary a lot of information was discussed. He said that they only ever raised one chick even if two eggs were laid. I remembered something about them looking after the chick for a long time and most photos of the nest seem to show an adult standing guard. They are the world's largest true raptor with a wingspan that reaches to just over three metres or ten feet! After he left, the German and Finnish couples that I had talked with on the castle stopped, I was able to show them the vultures through my binoculars.

There were Red-rumped Swallows catching insects over the water and further up the road I saw Bee-eaters and Azure-winged Magpies. Leaving Monfragüe, I crossed over to the southern flanks of the Sierra de Gredos and took up my 2015 route ('A Spanish Backbone'). On the other side of the Gredos runs the N-110 from Plasencia to Barco de Ávila through the Jerte valley, this is known as the Cherry Road. In late march or early april the mountainsides are white with blossom and the air scented. In summer during the harvest, everything is cherries. The main local *picota* cherry being especially sweet bought from a roadside stall. Be aware though that like any crop, bad weather at the wrong time can devastate the crop.

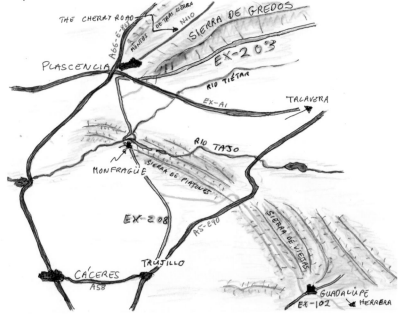

A Spanish Backbone

This section comprises a route from the Sierra de Gata on the Portuguese border to Riaza at the end of the Sierra Guadarrama, north of Madrid. Even if you can only fit a bit of it into your adventure I think you'll find it worthwhile. This was part of my June 2015 trip. I had been with friends close to Lisbon and was heading for Burgos, so I decided that a route as high up in the Sierras as possible might be fun, added to which it was getting into the mid-40°s in Portugal and the cool of mountains seemed a nice idea.

I arrived at the Gata campsite after about 6 hours of riding 360-odd kilometres. I was pleased to see that the campsite was by a river with reasonable pitches with hedges dividing them up.

It cost €10.50 for the one night, this comprised 3.50 for me, 3 for the *moto* and 4 for the tent. This slightly bizarre way of charging is common in Spanish campsites. In some cases if you are in a 'free' area, not on a pitch, they don't charge for the *moto*. There was the normal bar/restaurant on site, and another just outside, close to the river and the old stone bridge which crosses it. Nice rock pools and places to paddle or swim in cool mountain water. I sat in the river and rinsed my sweaty clothes. Later I got a fresh *bocadillo* and a *vaso de vino tinto* for supper and slept well, to memories of the gorgeous flash of brilliant yellow when a Golden Oriole flew across the road in front of me on my way from Penamacor.

I left the campsite just after 9am. A twisty road brought me down out of the mountains through Gata and Torre and out onto the plain bound for Plasencia. Flatter, long straights and the horizon a rim of lofty, hazy, mountains. Cork oak and olive groves, the predominate land use. The smell of Extremadura is dust and granite, Asturias, Galicia and much of Portugal the heavy scent of hot eucalyptus. The high Spanish mountains wash one with the fragrance of pine.

Not long after negotiating Plasencia one begins to climb up into the Sierra

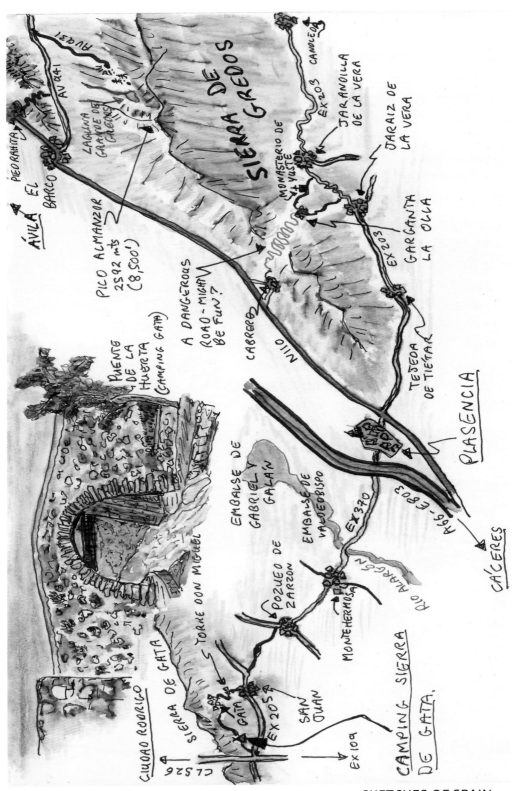

AV-Q31

AV Q-1

AVILA

PIEDRAHITA

EL BARCO

LAGUNA GRANDE DE GREDOS

SIERRA DE GREDOS

PICO ALMANZOR 2592 mts (8,500')

A DANGEROUS ROAD - MIGHT BE FUN?

CABRERO

NIÑO

PUENTE DE LA HUERTA (CAMPING GATA)

MONASTERIO DE YUSTE

EX-203

JARANDILLA DE LA VERA

JARAIZ DE LA VERA

GARGANTA LA OLLA

EX-203

CANDELEDA

EX-203

TEJEDA DE TIETAR

PLASENCIA

CÁCERES

A966-E803

CIUDAD RODRIGO

SIERRA DE GATA

TORRE DON MIGUEL

POZUELO DE ZARZON

EMBALSE DE GABRIEL Y GALAN

EMBALSE DE VALDEOBISPO

EX-370

RIO ALAGÓN

MONTEHERMOSA

GATA

EX-205

SAN JUAN

CL-526

EX-109

CAMPING SIERRA DE GATA.

de Gredos. Seeing a sign for Garganta de Olla after leaving Jaraiz I was intrigued. *Garganta* is a 'throat' but in place names will mean a *cañón* or gorge and an *olla* is a pot. It is off my intended route, a detour up into the mountains but the decision to explore only took a moment. The town is typical, the older part cosily surrounding the Plaza Mayor and church on a small eminence at the foot of the Sierra. At the far end of the town I spotted a *mini-supermercado* and stopped for information and some lunch supplies (*pan* - bread, *chorizo* and *queso* - cheese). I wandered in and was met with a cheerful *"Hola"* from the young man behind the counter whose ear was getting bent by an elderly lady.

I gathered my goods and the lady stepped back and slowed the gossip to let me make my purchases. In my very simple and bad Spanish I asked where the Garganta was - (*¿Dónde está la Garganta?*). Is it a canyon? (*¿Es un cañón?*). *"Si, es un cañón. Es muy bonito."* - It is very pretty. He gave me directions which I followed easily. Left - *izquierda*, right - *derecha*, straight on – *recto*. Soon I came to a car park above the Garganta Mayor or 'greater throat'. The river tumbles under a stone bridge into a long pool. I think I can see the *ollas* in the river bed; stone - ground potholes. There is a big parking area and an obvious swimming area, which I'm sure is very popular with the locals later in the day. The rushing little river comes dancing its way round

boulders and over little falls from a cool wooded valley that I would have liked to have had time to explore. Walking trails head up that way and I am sure the *cañón* would become more spectacular the higher you got. I was very pleased to have some nice views of a Dipper, flitting between boulders and bobbing up and down on the spot, in its characteristic manner. It's not much bigger than a Robin but has the ability to 'fly' underwater to get larvae from the riverbed.

It was time to move on and so I saddled up and headed on up the EX-391. It is a pretty, narrow and winding

road, sometimes agricultural, sometimes bare mountainside and forests. Very enjoyable. Suddenly I came into what seemed to be one big car park next to the grand Monasterio de Yuste. It is open Tuesday - Sunday between 10am and 7pm. Founded by Heironymite monks in 1402, it was made famous by Emperor Charles V who retired there in 1557. Certainly if you have the time and interest, it is worth taking in. Having negotiated the car park and found the continuation of the road, I followed it till it rejoined the EX-203 at the pretty little town of Caucos de Yuste. It would have made a nice lunch stop but I went onward.

This road has long straights and sweeping corners and great views with an open plain to the south which stretches away across the valley of the Rio Tajo to the distant Sierra de Guadalupe. To the north one keeps catching views of the impressive heights of the Gredos. Losar de la Vera has some interesting topiary... Just before Madrigal de la Vera I found a shady lay-by with tables, the peaks a backdrop. I was serenaded by the lovely churring song and brilliant flashes of colour from Bee-eaters and a very loud cicada

which it took me ages to spot. Onward in nice low 30°s, eventually to some nice curves coming to Arenas San Pedro with its impressive castle overlooking the town.

The ever looming mountains are a hazy backdrop. It is not far from Arenas to the Parador de Gredos. This was the first official parador and is

Peaks of the Sierra de Gredos (mid-June)

a favourite of mine. The standard of rooms in the paradors are always of the highest quality and the staff are friendly even to a sweaty biker. At this one, I arrived once and the receptionist recognised me from the one night I had stayed two years previously. It is beautifully situated in the high valley between the Sierra de Gredos and Sierra de Villafranca both of which rise to peaks over 6,500'. A walk up to the Laguna Grande de Gredos is well worthwhile, the massive ring of mountains curve round the lake, and big wild goats stare at you with their slitty golden eyes.

Anyway, back to Arenas where I decided to do some high passes. I headed north up the N-520 for a short way before turning off for San Esteban del Valle and Serranillos. This took me over the Puerto de Serranillos at 1575 mts (over 5,000'). Through Serranillos and onto Navarrevisca around a thousand feet lower and round to head back up and over the Puerto de Mijares again at 1570 mts. These are fantastic switch-back mountain roads with stunning views. When in the pine woods up here it's best to be on the look-out for huge pine cones in the road or gravel pushed into the inside of bends by corner-cutting Spanish drivers, another hazard, should you actually meet any up here. If you see a 20 kmph advisory sign before a bend I'd believe it! This detour was very much a challenge worth taking in my view, for the sights and smells of the broom flowers and cool pine glades around the slowly aging granite. Coming back down I passed through the little pueblo of Mijares and on to Casavieja. There is a very nice campsite here a little way out of the town up towards the mountains and amongst the pine woods, but I am headed for the Valle Enmedio site

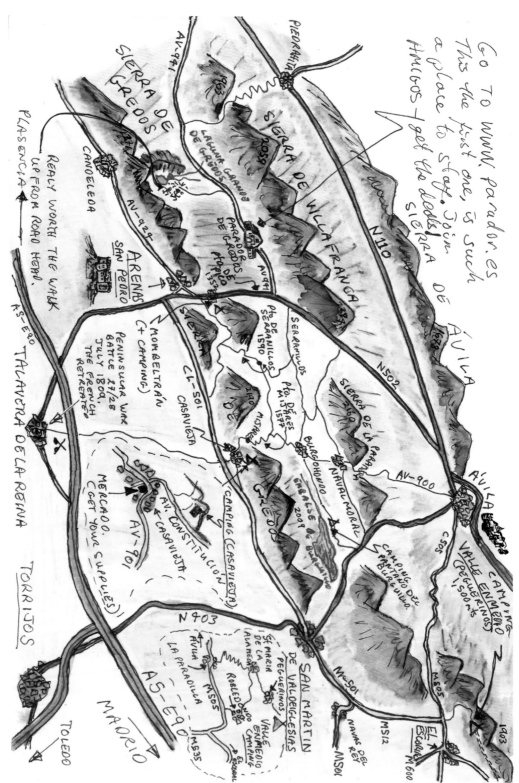

above El Escorial this time, so on towards Sotillo and San Martin.

The last time I had stayed in Valle Enmedio I arrived there on the high dirt road from the Puerto de Guadarrama and left it almost straight down into El Escorial. The trouble was, I couldn't remember where that route arrived in the town. So I visited the palace briefly and then set out to find my way up to Peguerinos, the *pueblo* before the campsite. This means heading toward Ávila on the M-505 but making sure to catch the small side road to Robledondo then Santa Maria de Alameda and wind, wind your way up to Peguerinos where you will find signs for the campsite. It was about 6.30 pm when I arrived after nearly 400 km of riding, over 9 hours. But what a wonderful experience, full of sights, sounds and smells, meeting people and immersing myself in España.

The delightful Rosario, who was manning reception welcomed me.

She later told me that the road down into El Escorial was worse than the one from the Puerto. I confirmed this by going down it in 2016, bad tarmac and potholes, grit and stones and some steep sections. Definitely coming through Robledondo was the best way. She assured me that many caravans and motorhomes did come up that way. The 'free' area for camping at the far end is very pleasant and totally empty at the end of June. I was glad I had brought a decent sleeping bag, as the temperature here at around 5,000' drops quite sharply at night. By the way, there is not a lot of mobile phone signal and no Wi-Fi, which one normally finds at every campsite (it might have changed by the time you get there). I quite enjoy that. To some extent I miss the old days when one's adventure was private, experienced as a whole before you told anyone about it and when one was free from emails and updates on the life temporarily left behind.

Rosario and I chatted, she in English whilst I replied whenever possible in Spanish. I treasure hearing about someone's kids and how they are growing up, little details of the differences in family and culture between Spain and the British.

I left Enmedio at 8.30 am the next morning taking the high road to the Puerto de Guadarrama. The big Stelvio is not really (at least for me) an off-roading bike. It weighs in at around 275 kg depending on how much fuel for the bike, or for me is on board (@650+lbs). This means picking it up, if dropped, is a little bit of a strain. However, there are no steep sections and it is really a case of dodging pine cones and big rocks whilst steering round the potholes. When I first found the campsite I did this road on my Guzzi Centauro, a much sportier, but lighter bike.

The views are worth it, particularly looking down into the Valle de Los Caidos (P 132). Once back to civilisation it is down the N-VI towards Madrid but only so I can get off onto the M-614 for Navacerrada. After which you could jump over to Segovia on the M-601 which will turn into the CL-601 as you crest the Puerto de Navacerrada at 1860 mts (over 6,000') or continue on the M-604 to Lozoya where, as you cross a bridge over a little river, you will find the main road bending right but to the left is the Plaza de Antonio Blanco and the M-637 for Navafria. On this little square is the Bar/Restaurante Serna, a pleasant square to sit with a *café solo* or a spot of lunch (*el almuerzo*) before the wondrous climb over Puerto de Navafria.

As you exit Lozoya you follow a ridge for a little while so it's fairly straight, then as you climb into the pines it gets more interesting. Bends can get a bit sharper and watch out for cyclists (damn, but the Spanish are fit), and cows who might think they own the road. At the top it might be 15° cooler than Lozoya, breathe that pine fresh air and listen for the wind, and the finches hidden in the pine tops.

On the way up here I had the joy of seeing a scampering, massive and beautiful black squirrel with a bushy full red tail, I was smiling for a long while after, and he lives bright in my memory.

Coming down from the pass is just as much fun as going up. At the bottom after you pass Navafria you hit the N-110. You could use this to go straight to the A1 or you could take another little detour and having gone right for a short way, turn off again onto the SG-V-2316 for Pedraza. In fact there are a couple of ways through, but this is probably the best. It is a very scenic, winding route though I have to say the road was a little lumpy last time I used it, but hey, it may have been re-surfaced by the time you get to it. After a while you come through sparse woodland alongside a *barranca* (mostly-dry riverbed) to where you come round a corner and ahead of you is the impressive castle and walls of Pedraza. It is well worth a visit, the

Pedraza

castle doors are really impressive. Enjoy the Plaza Mayor, the town is real 'Castilla' and being a bit off the main routes, is not spoilt and not touristy most of the time.

When you leave, you could go back to the N-110 and on to Riaza which I have made an arbitrary end point for this route, or take another detour and enjoy the beauties of the valley of the Rio Duratón and Sepúlveda. This means heading up to Cantalejo. From Pedraza you want to take the La Velilla (Segovia) road. In Rebollo watch for the turning to the left just as you enter, which takes you through the middle of the town and on to Cabezuela on the SG-V-2311 and then Cantalejo on the CL-603.

You might choose to go that way up to Aranda de Duero. Going to Aranda there are great long straights under a massive Castilian sky, then a dip into pine forests and perhaps a distant ridge crowned with wind turbines all stately waving you past.

In the middle of Cantalejo you come to a crossroads and for the Duratón you need to almost go back on yourself to take the SG-205 Sepúlveda road for a short while. But before you leave the town take the SG-V-2323 for Sebúcor, the most scenic route. After Sebúcor you will wind down into a riverside valley, this is the Rio San Juan. You have to go back up and over before the switchbacks that will bring you down into the quite deeply cut valley of the Rio Duratón.

Sepúlveda, when you get to it, is a nice place to stop for a coffee at the very least. I stayed there once with Spanish friends from Madrid in the small (13 room) Hostal El Mirador del Casilla. It has a very good restaurant 'El Alfoz' down below. The room rates are very good at currently around €35 for a single. Lovely rooms, nice view and parking outside, €4 optional breakfast. If you come to it along the Calle los Fueros and stop at the little Plaza Santiago you can park there and go up the steps to the street above, where the Hostal is located. You can see it from los Fueros but the Calle Conde it is on becomes pedestrian and is a bit tight. In the evening we walked into the town and by following people and sounds we found an event going on in the 'village hall',

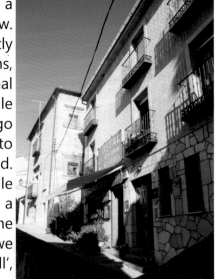

Hostal El Mirador del Casilla - Sepúlveda

where we squeezed onto a table for tapas, wine and talk whilst listening to the local band playing Spanish and Latin-American dance tunes. They were very good, and very smart in their costumes. Woodwind and some brass, all generations were present, occasionally kids particularly finding somewhere to dance a little. A thoroughly enjoyable evening, we didn't get back to the hostal till gone midnight.

I have to say the road at least as far as Sepúlveda was a little lumpy and single track at times, but it is fun... Leaving Sepúlveda, take the SG-233 but just as you arrive at El Olmo there is a bar all on its own in a triangle of road; you want to go right around the back of it to get on the SG-234 for Riaza, it claims to become the SG-911 before you pick up the N-100 for a bit before the signs for Riaza. Normal story; follow *centro urbano* or *ciudad* to arrive at the 'centre'!

It won't be long before you are in the striking Plaza Mayor. It is elliptical which is quite unusual, and has porticos and stone columns holding up overhanging balconies. The town is nestled hard up against the backbone of the Sierras, in this case the Sierra de Ayllón which is a continuation of the Guadarrama.

So maybe I'll say go as far as Ayllón before we end this route, to visit

Entrance to the old town of Ayllón

another small, out of the way and enchanting town. Of course ahead of you is Burgo de Osma and then my favourite Sierra de la Demanda.

Here I am distracted from the planned chapter end, because in 2006 during my 'Five Eagles Tour', Charlie, Richard and I caught a wedding in Burgo. We sat at a plaza table and became vicariously involved. As we settled in the plaza we soon became aware of a sense of anticipation, centred around the main church doors. We realised it was a wedding.

By the way, weddings are a massive thing in Spain, and very much a time for a very big extended family reunion and celebration. Usual thing, everyone was checking their watches and wondering when the bride and groom were coming out. Suspense mounted. At last out

they came to a barrage of rice and a serenade from a guitar player and singer. I think if we hadn't been on a schedule for the tour I would have struck up a crude conversation with the celebrants and we'd probably have been there all night. In this last photo one of the bridesmaids is trying to shake the rice out of her dress.

You can only happen upon these sorts of experiences by sheer serendipity; taking the back roads and making time for the smallest village, or a chance encounter. Something doesn't always come your way, but when it does it is memorable and enriching. If you decide to go round the world on your tricycle then a good way into the attitude required is a fortnight of absorbing and being absorbed into Spain. Learn that schedules are there to be broken. If you are gifted an experience, take it. Don't be a 'mile boaster'!

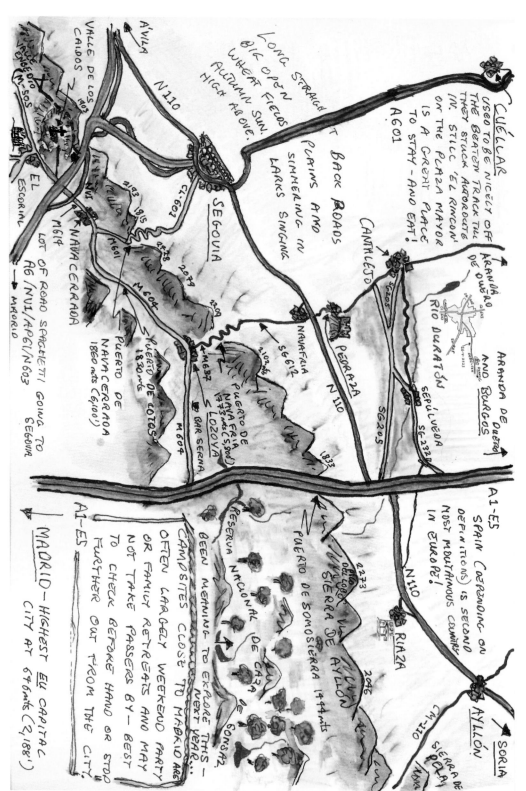

CUÉLLAR USED TO BE NICELY OFF THE BEATEN TRACK TILL THEY STUCK AUTOROUTE IN. STILL 'EL RINCON' ON THE PLAZA MAYOR IS A GREAT PLACE TO STAY - AND EAT!

LONG STRAIGHT BIG OPEN WHEAT FIELDS SIMMERING IN AUTUMN SUN. HIGH ABOVE.

T BACK ROADS PLAINS AND LARKS SINGING

A601

N110

CL601

ÁVILA

VALLE DE LOS CAÍDOS

EL ESCORIAL

M614

NAVACERRADA

2183   1915

M601

2079

M604

2209

art8

SEGOVIA

CANTALEJO

ARANDA DE DUERO

AND BURGOS

RIO DURATÓN

SG205

SG205

SEPÚLVEDA

SG-232P

NAVAFRÍA

SG612

N110

PEDRAZA

1833

PUERTO DE NAVACERRADA 1860 mts (6,100')

PUERTO DE COTOS

M637

2.102 mts

PUERTO DE NAVA FRÍA 1473 mts (5,900')

LOZOYA

BAR SERNA

M604

LOT OF ROAD SPAGHETTI GOING TO SEGOVIA
A6/NVI/AP61/N603

A6/NVI/AP61/N603 → MADRID

A1-ES

A1-ES

SPAIN (DEPENDING ON DEFINITIONS) IS SECOND MOST MOUNTAINOUS COUNTRY IN EUROPE!

N110

RIAZA

2046

SIERRA DE AYLLÓN

PICO DEL LOBO 2273

RESERVA NACIONAL DE CAZA

PUERTO DE SOMOSIERRA 1444 mts

RESERVA NACIONAL DE CAZA DE SONSAZ

BEEN MEANING TO EXPLORE THIS - NEXT YEAR...

CAMPSITES CLOSE TO MADRID ARE OFTEN LARGELY WEEKEND PARTY OR FAMILY RETREATS AND MAY NOT TAKE PASSERS BY - BEST TO CHECK BEFORE HAND OR STOP FURTHER OUT FROM THE CITY.

A1-ES → MADRID - HIGHEST EU CAPITAL CITY AT 676mts (2,188')

AYLLÓN

SORIA

SIERRA DE POLA

Peñafiel

Peñafiel is located halfway between Aranda de Duero and Valladolid on the N-122. If coming from Burgos I like getting there by a rather zigzag route, heading first toward Soria on the N-234 and taking in Mercerres and Covarrubias, and/or the Garganta de Yecla at St Domingo de Silos. Find Pinilla-Trasmonte where there is a pretty little bridge and picnic spot by the river and passing through Pineda-Trasmonte, duck under the A-1 Burgos-Madrid *autovia* and use the BU-130 which will take you past yet another interesting town perched on a bluff above the Duero river. Roa de Duero has a lovely Plaza Mayor by the church, oh dear yet another coffee stop required. Whichever way you come to Peñafiel at a turn in the road you will suddenly see the spectacular castle, standing proud on its boat-shaped cliff. It is an extraordinary natural feature crowned by a magnificent construction taking full defensive advantage of the steep sides of the

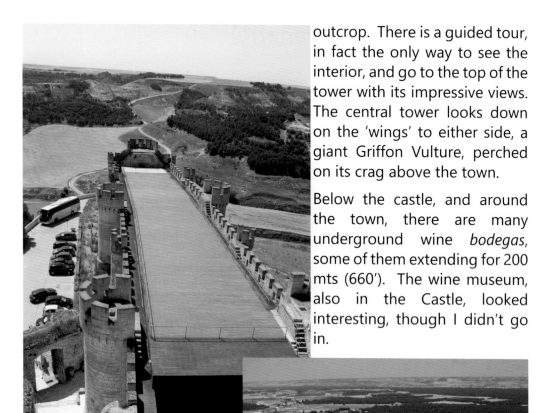

outcrop. There is a guided tour, in fact the only way to see the interior, and go to the top of the tower with its impressive views. The central tower looks down on the 'wings' to either side, a giant Griffon Vulture, perched on its crag above the town.

Below the castle, and around the town, there are many underground wine *bodegas*, some of them extending for 200 mts (660'). The wine museum, also in the Castle, looked interesting, though I didn't go in.

The medieval Plaza del Coso in the town has been used for bullfights from its earliest days and the normally private balconies around it are auctioned by the *Ayuntamiento* - Town Hall, for events.

This is the province of Valladolid whose food is characterised by roasted meat of all kinds.

Chuletones de Buey is a speciality of Peñafiel, a large ox steak with *ajillo* - garlic.

Cuéllar

28 km south-west of Peñafiel is the town of Cuéllar. Use the VA-233/SG-233 and there is a 20 km straight. Coming the other way you become aware of the Peñafiel castle which then steadily grows as you head endlessly toward it.

Though probably going back to the 10th century, it was in the 13th that it really grew and became an important royal city. As with Burgos, a lot of the wealth was due to the wool trade. It has a castle and many medieval buildings. It also has a very ancient 'Running of the Bulls' fiesta, which is probably

pagan and is thought to be the oldest in Spain. In 1215, priests were forbidden to join in the running. It is celebrated for 5 days, from the last Saturday of August.

I stayed a very enjoyable night here in 2006 at La Hostería Restaurante el Rincón Castellano (above) which is on the Plaza Mayor. My little balcony looked down on the bikes and the room was very comfortable and full of character with exposed beams It has an excellent restaurant down below and is centrally located for exploring the town.

Segovia

At Segovia I usually make my way around to the foot of the magnificent Roman aqueduct, built in the first century AD. It was still in use in the 1980's. There is a wide plaza in front of it and you can park your bike up with all the others in the bike park that has been set up. A great example of a bit of Spanish common sense, in years gone by all the bikes were randomly parked on the pavement off the roundabout, now the city has it nicely organised. You can then sit at the nearby restaurant or café tables within sight of your bike and enjoy a *café solo* whilst you contemplate the genius of Roman construction. Mind you I reckon it is pretty safe with all the other bikers watching. So take a walk up the pedestrian streets beyond the aqueduct. If you go up the streets trending right you will get to the Plaza Mayor and the great Gothic cathedral. There are a number of things to see and the city is small enough to be easy to get around.

The Alcazar is particularly impressive and dates from the 1100's and has been popular with later monarchs who added to it. A bad fire in 1862 means a lot of reconstruction has been done.

The first Spanish Military Academy the Royal School of Artillery, was inaugurated at Segovia in 1764, and is still based here.

Only 17 km from the city centre is the Peñalara peak at 2429 mts (nearly 8,000′) and the highest point of the Sierra de Guadarrama.

One of the joys of riding the N-110 to Segovia and on to Ávila is the views of the imposing wall of the Sierra. Until early summer one can often still see snow on the highest peaks.

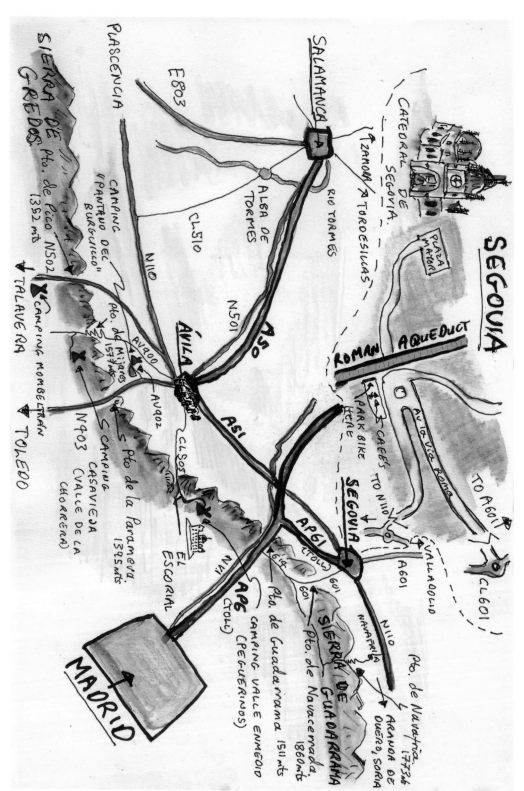

El Escorial

I always try and find the time to visit El Escorial between Ávila and Segovia. The corner stone was laid in 1563 for King Philip II who saw it as a central part of his fight against the Protestant Reformation. It is much more than just a royal palace with a basilica, convent, school, library, and the resting place for Spanish Monarchs. There is a timelessness to its architecture which, particularly from the outside, seems very modern in its austerity. Out front there is a large pond with really huge carp in it. I have spent a happy half hour watching a Grey Heron looking for the small fry whilst dodging the monster carp who roil the surface if anyone throws in some bread.

As in many places in Spanish towns there are wide pavements and at the corner where the Paseo de Carlos III bends around the Parque Almirante Carrero Blanco toward the palace, you can easily slip the *moto* out of pedestrian's way by the wall; look over it and you will be above the pond and have a great view of the front of the palace.

There is an enormous amount of the history of Spain to find here, and when you need a break walk up into to the town above where there are leafy squares, nice shops and great restaurants.

From El Escorial there are a number of ways to or from Segovia. Over the Puerto de Guadarrama (about 5,000'), going by the Toll AP-61 at 55 km - 50 mins, or the N-110 at 65 km, just over the hour. If you like a scenic route, go over the Puerto de Navacerrada. The latter is on mountain roads that wind up and up through the scented pine woods and it will take you at least an hour and a half depending on how often you stop; there are places you can take in the might of the mountain wall around Madrid.

The Guadarrama at this point is only 20-30 km wide but goes up to 2428 mts (nearly 8,000'). El Escorial like Segovia is at around 1000 mts (3,000'), so the wall is 4-5,000' high. Standing looking along the wall, I have become aware of a distant sound that grows and grows as it rushes towards me, the susurration of thousands of pine needles before a wind-wave sweeping the wall and eventually washing over me. It is a good place to spend time with the binoculars scanning the sky, as it is here that I have most often seen the Spanish Imperial Eagle.

There was fierce fighting in the defence of Madrid during the Civil War along these ridges. In winter the conditions for the soldiers must have been appalling.

By the way the campsite at El Escorial is one of those, and there are a number surrounding Madrid (and other big cities), that is used a lot for parties during summer weekends. You may well get invited to join in but expect it to be quite noisy. The time I stayed there I arrived on a Friday afternoon and the place was empty (bare earth and very few trees). I set up my tent in a corner. The first arrivals in the late afternoon, in a very Spanish way set up close to me (rather than at a distance as any self-respecting Brit would have done).

Valle de Los Caídos

Between El Escorial and the Puerto de Guadarrama there is a hidden valley; Valle de Los Caídos - the Valley of the Fallen. It is a controversial monument for many Spanish. Franco (a fascist) who won the Civil War and ruled Spain into the 1970s claimed it was a "national act of atonement and reconciliation" but many see it as a fascist monument. Franco is buried in the basilica though there has been pressure to remove him from the valley to try and lessen the link with his authoritarian regime and the Falangist/ fascist movements. The forestry road that one can take from Camping Valle Enmedio to the Puerto de Guadarrama affords one of the few views possible without paying to enter the valley. The cross in the valley is 150 mts (500') high.

Ávila

Ávila like Segovia is an easy lunch or afternoon stop point, even if one can't afford the time to stay over.

Ávila is unusual in that the castle walls are undamaged and still enclose the main city. The walls line the top of the hill on which the city stands and are not obscured by more recent buildings, and the old town inside the walls is very largely unspoilt.

The walls were begun in around 1090 after the Reconquista reached here and the Moors were pushed out. Ávila is famous for Santa Teresa de Jesús who lived here for much of her life and died in 1582. Most of October is given over to the Fiestas de Santa Teresa. The city was important and prosperous in the 16th century but during the 17th it declined until at one point it only had about 4,000 residents. This may well have been the saving of its spectacular walls. It was not important enough to warrant much fighting over, its walls would have stood little chance against the artillery of the 18th and 19th centuries.

It is interesting to compare it with the fortifications of Jaca, Ciudad Rodrigo and Almeida all designed and built to stand the best chance of surviving battering by cannon balls. In contrast they have no vertical walls easy to target for a breach but long grassy slopes to try and bounce the balls over the walls which though low, are protected by deep moats and ravelins.

I love to see those great walls rising from the bleak stony country that surrounds it, the Sierra de Gredos or Guadarrama looming in the distance. I always ride up toward the Arco San Vicente, the main gateway into the en-

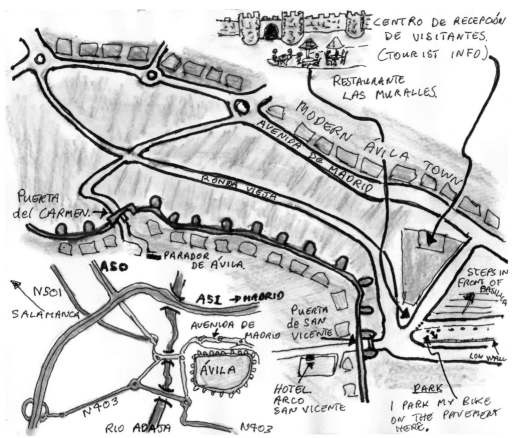

The map contains the following labels:

CENTRO DE RECEPCIÓN DE VISITANTES. (TOURIST INFO)

RESTAURANTE LAS MURALLES.

MODERN ÁVILA TOWN

AVENIDA DE MADRID

RONDA VIEJA

PUERTA del CARMEN. →

A50

N501 SALAMANCA

PARADOR DE ÁVILA.

A51 → MADRID

AVENIDA DE MADRID

PUERTA de SAN VICENTE

ÁVILA

N403

RIO ADAJA   N403

HOTEL ARCO SAN VICENTE

STEPS IN FRONT OF BASILICA

LOW WALL

PARK
I PARK MY BIKE ON THE PAVEMENT HERE.

castled old town. Just opposite there is the Basilica de San Vicente which has a big expanse of steps leading down to it with a narrow one-way road at the top. There is a low wall dividing it from the road above and enough pavement to park a *moto*. Having seen Spanish *motos* and scooters parked there I follow suit, and have never had a problem. VERY conveniently, just across the road is the Restaurante las Muralles (of the walls) just the place to sit for some light refreshment or the *menu del dia*.

One of the special things for me is the sight and sounds of the myriad swifts as they scream physically and aurally around the walls. Probably picking off flying ants. They show such sheer delight in their own abilities; wings like knife blades that can power them at amazing speed. They dice the very air as they cut

ÁVILA.

each other up, groups criss-crossing the sky, seemingly always in danger of collision, but it never happens.

I have stayed in the parador here, the impressive 16th century palace Piedras Albas. It is easy to find as it is just inside the walls through the Puerta del Carmen. I was able to park my *moto* under the reception window so it was safe. Another time I stayed in the Hotel Arco San Vicente which was very reasonable and pleasant. It has a garage and the bar next door is very friendly and open quite late. There are of course many other hotels and hostals in the town and if you go to the Centro de Recepción they will help you book somewhere.

Although the Michelin maps show the sign for a municipal campsite (2014) it had been closed for a number of years. In the section on campsites you will find details of the nearest that I know about and the map of the general area shows the locations. There are campsites along the Embalse de Burguillo south of Ávila toward the Sierra de Gredos.

Ávila is nicely situated to be fitted into north - south routes through the middle of Spain or those heading for mid or southern Portugal.

Ávila - The Catholic church of San Vicente opposite the imposing Arco de San Vicente (right). Where I park my bike on the pavement by the low wall.
The whole old town is still ringed by these impressive walls.

PAMPLONA
(N-240)
NOW A-21
N-121
A12
TAFALLA
NA-132
OLITE
LOGROÑO
LODOSA
PERALTA
NA-624
NA-128
MONASTERIO
DE LA OLIVA
SÁDAB
N-232
NA-125
TUDELA
ALFARO
N-113
SORIA
N-122
N-122
N-234
AP-68

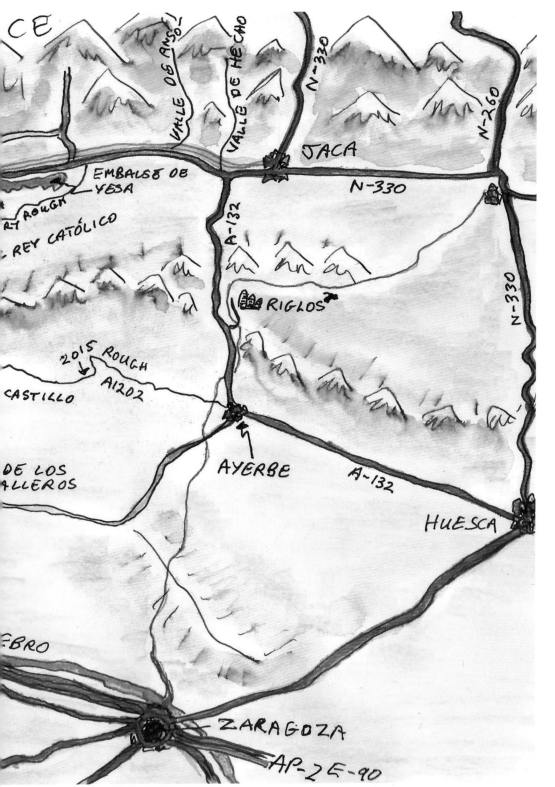

Olite

Olite is a small town but one well worth visiting for its 14th century medieval fortress which has an abundance of towers and courtyards, staircases and battlements. You can tell it was more of a 'folly' or display of grandeur because most, if not all the spiral staircases are anti-clockwise going up. Easier to climb with your hand on the rail but also easier to attack upwards

with a sword in the right hand. Defensive staircases are clockwise so that the defender has the right-handed advantage.

It also has the advantage of a nice restaurant for a cold beer, right on the square close to the castle. The Parador here is impressive being the palace part of the castle, with many medieval features. In the town there are narrow old streets and an area with roman walls. In the second week of August there is a spectacular Medieval Festival.

The NA-5303 and then the NA-132 to Sangüesa is a great road for a motorcyclist, on that tour I let everyone go as fast as they wanted, meeting up again just outside Sangüesa. The N-330 skirting the Embalse de Yesa toward Jaca was also a great road though they have been building a new *Autovia*, the A-21 from Pamplona and may have ruined it. If it's still there though, the old 'N' road will be even more enjoyable for having less traffic.

One of the things I most enjoy about this area of Spain is the constant presence of the Pyrenees. Whether glimpsed as a dark backdrop or perhaps imposing their strength early in the morning, when the air is crisp and clean and they seem to have strode closer during the night.

Once, riding the N-330, out of the corner of my eye I became aware of a big bird cruising almost level with me. I did keep eyes on the road, honest... It was my first sighting of a Lammergeier, a vulture that has managed to assume culture and lost its vulture name (Bearded Vulture), in favour of something grander. For many heartbeats we flew side by side, perhaps ten metres apart. I envied his 'tache'.

An Olite palace turret.

Sos del Rey Católico

Forty-odd kilometres to the west along the Sierra is Sos del Rey Católico, the Rey Católico bit being added after the birth here of King Ferdinand II (1452). The centre has not changed much since then, probably because it is in the middle of nowhere. The roads to it are in the process of being upgraded but in 2015 I found one of the worst stretches of so called tarmac road I have ever encountered. On a day which began in the Sierra de la Demanda and included Riglos I had ridden about 460 km, the temperature was up in the thirties and then I hit the A-1601 for the last 40 km from the east end of the Embalse de Yesa to Sos del Rey. Great scenery, but the tarmac was a random mess of potholes, gravel, lumps and short stretches that were fine, but lulled one into a speed that would suddenly be curtailed by the next hazard.

It was late afternoon when I got there and I was knackered. I pulled up at the Parador de Sos del Rey Católico hoping that I could talk them into a cheap room; they did knock off €20 but it was still €100 for the night.

I should have gone looking for somewhere cheaper but I was just too tired and so succumbed. The parador is very nice, and though not ancient, is very tasteful.

The streets of the town are 'donkey' streets though the locals manage to get vehicles through some of them, and there are good places to eat and other hotels and hostals. The ancient stone buildings, narrow alleys and small squares have a wonderful feeling of history.

The best road in and out is undoubtedly the A-127, Sangüesa to the north and Ejea to the south. The A-1202 from Unacastillo to Ayerbe also being pretty rough in 2015.

Travelling from Burgos to this area I probably use the N-120 till Logroño. But then find the NA-624 on the north side of the Ebro, the motorways run on the south side. Going through Lodosa and Peralta keeps one on sweeping empty country roads that are a pleasure. And you can use the NA-115 to get from Peralta to Olite, again dodging motorways. Out of Olite start off on the NA-5303 until it joins the NA-132 at San Martín de Unx if you are going via Sangüesa.

Views at the top of the town

Jaca

I have been through and stayed in Jaca a few times, and always enjoyed the small town feel of the place. Often this has been when crossing the French border as it is a good stopping point before or after crossing the Pyrenees.

There are many passes, but if you start at the Biscay end it is about number three of the main ways over. If you have been doing France as fast as possible you will cross the border with the motorways at Hendaye/Irun.

The next main one eastward is the Camino de Santiago pass from St Jean-Pied-a-Port to Roncevalles. You could have sliced off at Biarritz to come this way and St Jean is pretty and the pass above great. Roncevalles is of course connected with the ballad of noble Roland and the battle that took place in 778. Rather typically the 'spin doctors' got to work on what was a disaster really for Charlemagne who had said he was fighting the Muslims but had plundered several Pyrenean towns and pretty much destroyed Pamplona. As a result a Basque army attacked and wiped out his rearguard as it was going through the pass back to France. Roland, the Prefect of Brittany was one of the commanders of the rearguard but was too proud to call for reinforcements from the main army until it was too late. He was written up as the brave hero! The N-135 between Espinal and Zubiri is pretty spectacular but then you have to go round Pamplona, which may or may not be to your liking.

For Jaca you would come from Pau and Oloron Ste. Marie which for me works with a French route from Poitiers/Limoges avoiding going to sleep on the coastal motorway. There is now the 8.6 km Somport tunnel that takes a lot of the climbing out of the pass. It is an 'experience', particularly on a motorbike. I went through and did not see another vehicle, just a seemingly endless orange worm-hole. I was quite glad not to find myself on Aldebran when I finally came out into fresh air. One can find the old road though and take in a nice bit of mountain scenery.

There are a number of other smaller but exciting passes, it just depends on the scale of your map how many you can find. Despite looking from a distance like an impenetrable wall, the Pyrenees have always been well crossed and of course the Basques reckon to own both sides. The Nazis never stoppered all the holes, which leaked escapees throughout the Second World War... Going further east to Andorra and beyond there are many more ways across - on my list of things to do.

In Jaca I stay in the Hotel Boira. A very friendly, pleasant little hotel which has a garage you can put a *moto* in and perhaps a car if you ask beforehand. The 11th century Romanesque Cathedral (it's not that big) is worth a visit and the castle is very impressive. 16th century, it embodies the anti-artillery architecture of sloping glacis and deep moat. Look for the Rock Sparrows if you like birds and sometimes there are pretty deer in the moat. And, If you are interested militaria there is an amazing collection of lead miniatures on dioramas in the museum housed in the Citadel.

Riglos

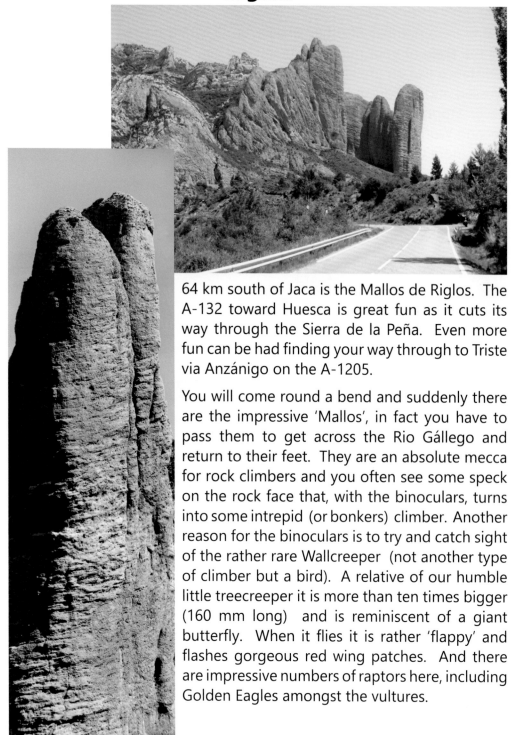

64 km south of Jaca is the Mallos de Riglos. The A-132 toward Huesca is great fun as it cuts its way through the Sierra de la Peña. Even more fun can be had finding your way through to Triste via Anzánigo on the A-1205.

You will come round a bend and suddenly there are the impressive 'Mallos', in fact you have to pass them to get across the Rio Gállego and return to their feet. They are an absolute mecca for rock climbers and you often see some speck on the rock face that, with the binoculars, turns into some intrepid (or bonkers) climber. Another reason for the binoculars is to try and catch sight of the rather rare Wallcreeper (not another type of climber but a bird). A relative of our humble little treecreeper it is more than ten times bigger (160 mm long) and is reminiscent of a giant butterfly. When it flies it is rather 'flappy' and flashes gorgeous red wing patches. And there are impressive numbers of raptors here, including Golden Eagles amongst the vultures.

The Monasterio de la Oliva is a Cistercian monastery with about twenty monks in residence. It is on the NA-128 that can take you from Peralta to Sábada and you can visit and experience not only the historic building but gain a sense of the spirituality that moves these people listening to the monks chanting of liturgies.

The Valle de Hecho (pronounced 'Echo') is very well worth a visit and is another especially good place for the Wallcreeper. The A-176 from Puente la Reina de Jaca will take you up to the town of Hecho, and beyond up into the Parque Natural Valles Occidentales.

There are many places to visit along the Pyrenees towards Andorra. Most especially the Catalan Pyrenees. An area of amazing mountain roads, small and interesting towns with a wealth of different activities available, depending on the season. Rafting. Canoeing, Rock Climbing. Walking, Skiing...

Barcelona

I have to say that I have not been here on my *moto*. I was providing an American millionaire with a short guided tour across Europe. Wales, Zurich and Athens were also on the agenda; one of the compensations for the uncertainty of life as a self-employed 'Jack Of All Trades'.

Even before my American declared an interest in Gaudí I was fascinated by his architecture and had visited 'El Caprico' at Comillas close to Santander. Built between 1883-5, it includes double-glazing! It is particularly decorative. What you can see in Barcelona is the evolution of his ideas and his genius, the pre-eminent being the Cathedral of Sagrada Família. Construction had begun when he became Head Architect in 1883 but he made it his own and worked on it up until his death in 1926; it is still under construction.

I expect many people may find his work over-elaborate but what fascinates me is his attention to detail and construction. He studied natural forms to understand where the strength comes from in a tree for instance. This study of natural form allowed him to design in his unorthodox and organic style. Nature is mirrored in stone. The balconies on the Casa Milá are like the cliff ledges one sees in the *cañóns* of the Ebro. Columns are like tree trunks and tiles like leaves.

You won't regret a visit to Park Güell, the Cripta de la Colònia Güell and Sagrada Família. It is quite easy to walk up to the Park Güell from the Ramblas and gain a bit of height to look back over the city.

As a contrast, hidden in the back streets of the old town down by the sea is the Basilica de Santa Maria del Mar which has an incredible sense of space, light, and peace. Do read Ildefonso Falcones 'The Cathedral of the Sea', that tells its story.

Okay, the Ramblas is THE place for partying and this city can be very hedonistic.

It is well worth venturing away from the Ramblas which is very much the tourist centre of the city with hundreds of bars and restaurants, they are expensive. However later at night it may not be such a good idea to wander deep into the side streets and alleyways close to the Ramblas. There is a certain amount of potential for pickpockets etc, with so many tourists, some of them very drunk.

If you walk away from the sea up the Ramblas you will hit the Avenida Diagonal (it slashes diagonally across the city). Beyond this, though now subsumed into the city are once independent villages and they retain much of that feel, you will find very good food a lot cheaper.

Having said that I did eat (on the American) at a great restaurant in the Marina. We had a traditional speciality *calçots*; Leeks in Romesco sauce. The leeks are grown in a special way so that they are very soft and white. As soon as you order it the waiter brings a bib to put on your front because the technique of eating them is to lift the

Basilica de Santa Maria del Mar

dripping leek above your head with your fingers, before lowering it into your mouth.! Great fun.

There is also the cable car to Montjuic, a certain famous football club stadium and then if you have wheels, the Costa Dorada and Brava to be explored.

Do be careful of your vehicle and belongings. In particular hired campers or cars that are obviously being used by tourists can be a target for criminals looking for passports and cameras.

Park Güell

Alcorisa and Calanda

In 2002 I heard that the Moto Guzzi Club of Spain were having their annual rally at a place called Alcorisa. I decided to go, I would have time, just; four days in UK and ferry travel, three days in Spain, two nights at the rally.

This was only my third year of *moto* trips to Spain so I was not as confident as I am now, but it was a very good experience that stretched my comfort boundaries and taught me a lot about what one can achieve in friendship and communication in a 'foreign' land.

I took the N-234 from Burgos, past Soria and on to Calatayud. Next Daroca tucked up against the hills. Just after Calamocha I turned left onto the N-211 which would take me all the way Alcorisa.

Montalbán is about halfway, a small town backed up against the foot of the Sierra de San Just, with a surprisingly large church, the Iglesia del Apóstol Santiago. A very interesting mix of Mudéjar and Gothic.

Cruising onward the vegetation was getting significantly less, the air dryer and hotter. After Los Olmos it began to feel quite *desierto*. After 400 km plus, I arrived at Alcorisa.

It needed a few "*¿dónde está... ?*" to find the hostal. I took a deep breath and entered, knowing that there might not be anyone who spoke any English and my Spanish was very poor. But there was the welcoming Carlos 'Guttenburg' and his wife and son. We had corresponded after a fashion by email, so I wasn't a total surprise. As it turned out, there were no English speakers

until the last day but in the meantime I just had to do my best. It was a very friendly crowd, who went out of their way to include me. There were about twenty-five men, women and a few kids. All the men slept in one big dormitory, which was fine apart from the one guy who snored like a hippo in a chocolate cake! Main meals were included in the registration fee, and taken at one big table; three courses and vast quantities of wine, water and *casera*. La Casera is a rather sweet fizzy soda that many Spanish add to *vino de mesa* - table wine, the stuff that can be a little rough...

We had a big parade around the town led by the Guardia Civil. Down streets that nearly had their wing mirrors brushing the walls, and were cobbled and sloped to a central gutter, the slow speed riding was interesting. The noise from all those big 'V' Twins was ear-numbing, but the locals waved and cheered as we all went past. Then the Guardia led us out of town and through country that became more and more like a scene from the Wild West, cacti and dull sand, hot flinty air and the exhausts booming off rock walls. We rode past a deep blue *embalse*, and up, and up, a winding mountainous road. And came to a sudden halt. The Guardia apparently had a route in mind down the other side of the pass, the problem being pointed out to them was that a steep, stony, grit strewn dirt road was going to be a recipe for disaster for twenty-odd road bikes. A laborious turnaround and we trundled back down on tarmac. Then there was the reception provided by the town (with nibbles) and a speech by the Mayor.

Alcorisa is a really pleasant, out of the way town, a fascinating church tower, houses built into the high cliffs above, and when I was there a Golgotha-like trio of big crosses on the skyline above the town. Just up the road

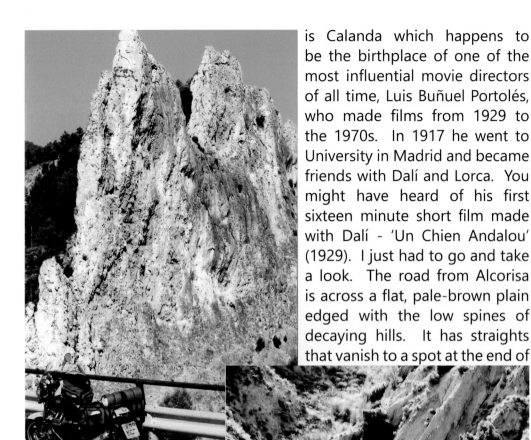

is Calanda which happens to be the birthplace of one of the most influential movie directors of all time, Luis Buñuel Portolés, who made films from 1929 to the 1970s. In 1917 he went to University in Madrid and became friends with Dalí and Lorca. You might have heard of his first sixteen minute short film made with Dalí - 'Un Chien Andalou' (1929). I just had to go and take a look. The road from Alcorisa is across a flat, pale-brown plain edged with the low spines of decaying hills. It has straights that vanish to a spot at the end of your vision which encourages a motorcyclist's right wrist to twist down, more, and more, until 200 kmph seems like a good enough point to slacken off.

The scenery in this area of the Desierto de Calanda is not as extreme as around Tabernas. It is more of a high desert, I guess. Certainly quite unique and different from other parts of northern Spain. Well worth a visit.

Spanish Moments

Idly chatting with my friend Anna whose family runs the Hostal Acuarela, just off the Plaza de Espana. I was turning the pages of Diario de Burgos, the local newspaper when a headline caught my eye *'Voces de Galesas en el espolón'* - Welsh voices'? The picture below showed the Aberystwyth University Madrigal Singers! Reading the article, it seemed they were here to do a concert in the Iglesia Santa María la Real y Antigua de Gamonal.

LA IMAGEN   conecta@diariodeburgos.es

VOCES GALESAS EN EL ESPOLÓN

Estos jóvenes, pése a que sus camisetas rojas nos lo hicieran pensar, no están defendiendo la candidatura de Burgos 2016. Pertenecen al coro de la Universidad de Aberystwyth, en Gales (Gran Bretaña). Ofrecerán un recitan mañana a las 20.15 horas en la Real y Antigua de Gamonal. Ayer ensayaban a capela (y sonaba muy bien) en el Paseo del Espolón, con gorrilla incluida. FOTO: LUIS LÓPEZ ARAICO

It was very amusing later that evening as I checked into the Hostal Acanto in Gamonal (also run by Anna's family) and found the reception area full of the 'Mad Singers'. I really enjoyed the moment when I said I was from Aberystwyth. That evening I went into town with them on the Gamonal bus. They were going to do some busking on the *paseo* along by the river. They soon gathered an appreciative audience from the passers-by. As is normal in Burgos, everybody was strolling up and down and meeting friends. A number of small kids sat cross-legged in front of the singers and listened intently. They were singing capella but with a big variety of arrangements from medieval to modern. I talked to various Spanish people explaining that the group were from my home town in Wales, and promoting their concert the next day. They received a lot of coins in appreciation. Around 8pm I took them to 'Pecaditos' on the edge of the Plaza Mayor where you choose from a list of drinks and tapas all at €1. An hour or so later as we were crossing the Plaza towards El Cid and the bus back to Gamonal, they decided to do a bit more singing.

There was lots of *gente* passing through, but once they stood and started singing, an audience quickly gathered. Aged from 2 to 80, they listened as the singers voices filled this wonderful square. The 'new' plaza has long marble benches that were soon occupied. Every song was applauded, and at the end they sang an arrangement of 'Bridge over Troubled Waters'. I noticed a big, tough, working class sort of guy on the end of the bench had tears running down his face. It may have been a personal cathartic moment but it was also a very Spanish moment; these are a people who can let go, submerse themselves in the moment and the emotions that are present. Whether a bull-fight, flamenco or a group of young people singing in harmony. In a way I think that the 'harmony' was one of the strongest factors. That this group of youngsters were singing so tightly together, resonates so much with the Spanish sense of community and of shared endeavour. We caught a late bus back to Hostal Acanto. The concert in the Iglesia went off exceptionally well. The Renaissance pieces and hymns really suited the acoustics and made for a very powerful experience. Standing ovations! Well done the Mad Singers of Aberystwyth.

Salamanca 2014. I was staying with a family whilst doing my unsuccessful Super Intensive Spanish course. Every morning the *señora* would give me my breakfast whilst the TV news was on. That week happened to be the Pamplona Fiesta de San Fermin or the running of the bulls. I was amazed at the live coverage with slow-mo re-runs of people getting nobbled by the poor bulls, and was even more surprised by the 'expert' opinions on deaths and injuries. A sudden, very clear indicator of the difference in attitudes. In the UK the action would have been hidden, but the presenters would have tried to find someone to ask, "How do you feel?" (That your partner has just been gored or trampled to death)!

<u>Leaving Madrid 2014</u>. I decided on a whim to take a detour and turned off the A1 onto the N-320 to Torrelaguna. The CM-1002 was particularly good and after Casa de Uceda the CM-1052 which took me up to the Embalse de El Atazar via the mysterious Pontón de la Oliva. It's mysterious because although there is talk of an *embalse*, there isn't one.

Some research gave me this mangled translation of the Spanish entry in Wikipedia: "The Pontón de la Oliva is a dam Spanish, now in disuse, located in the Sierra de Ayllón, northeast of the Community of Madrid and northwest of the province of Guadalajara. The dam is the sixth and last with which is Lozoya River in its course, and in turn is the oldest (built in 1857) of the entire system of dams and channels of Canal de Isabel II, network

supplies drinking water to the capital of Spain and much of the community. The next dam is the Navalejos old, located six kilometres upstream. In 1848, reigning in Spain Isabel II, Madrid had 206,000 inhabitants, a number that grew quickly given its status as capital of the Kingdom. Except for a minority of privileged itself had water in their homes, the rest of the locals stocked up on the spurting from 54 sources and distributed 920 water carriers. All of it came from the water travel, consisting of qanats built in the Middle Ages (are mentioned in the charter of 1202) and extended successively until the nineteenth century and draining aquifers to bring water to the city."

A very interesting find. The main thing though was the great roads, curving views, mountains, cliffs and pines. The Embalse de El Atazar was very impressive and I very much enjoyed the sweeps of clean tarmac taking me up to El Berrueco, from where I rode to Lozoyela and got back onto the A1 for Burgos. Back on plan, minor detour...

The joys of one's own timetable and not abiding by a SatNav or PLAN.

2007. On the other hand there are times when the input of another has advantageous consequences. In 2007 I had met Nick on the ferry and we rode together off and on during our respective journeys. We were exploring the area north of Burgos between Frias and Briviesca. Frias has a

Frias

great castle perched above the town which we enjoyed exploring. Leaving there, I pulled us over to investigate the fascinating Ermita de Santa María de la Hoz at Tobera. Close by there are the *cascades* or waterfalls. Nick confessed he wouldn't have stopped. A little later on it was his turn. He was leading and took a dead end road up to the Santuario de Santa Casilda, I wouldn't have bothered. The chapel and buildings were fascinating, particularly the intricately painted ceiling. La Hospedería, a small hotel, looks wonderful and the restaurant top class.

The story of Santa Casilda is a curious one as she was the daughter of the Sultan of Toledo and a Muslim. She took pity on the Sultan's Christian prisoners taking them food and medicines. Amongst the prisoners were monks and priests and after a while, she converted secretly to Christianity. She is known as Casilda of the Roses because her father became suspicious that she was succouring the prisoners and one day returned unexpectedly

catching her with her skirts full of what he was sure was food and medicine. But when she was forced to show what she had they had miraculously turned into a bunch of roses. When the Sultan had gone, they turned back into food and medicine.

Casilda became ill and it was suggested that a remedy of bathing in the cold lakes of San Vicente near Briviesca might cure her. She travelled north and after being cured she decided to devote herself to God and refused to return to Toledo. She won the affection of the locals who she helped and they decided to build her a house to live in. Every time they put something together the angels came in the night and shifted it onto the top of the little mountain nearby. So they figured the *santuario* better be there. Round the corner was

a beautiful *burro*. I was glad Nick took me there. A lovely spot and one to stay at for a few days, walking and enjoying the surrounding area.

Portugal 2016.

Visiting my friends north of Braga I was invited to go along to a local *festa*. In a small village a stage was set up by the church, the local police were there to control traffic. There was a Scout band with huge, very loud drums and some brass, and two traditional dance troupes who each had in addition their own musicians with drums and accordions. There was lots of music and every now and then a thunder-flash rocket would explode overhead.

After everybody had marched up and down the road a bit with the Scouts doing some formation marching and playing round the church, the dancing on stage got underway. It was very hot, 45° degrees where I was, in a slight bit of shade. Probably nearer 50° on-stage!

It wasn't surprising that four of the dancers went down with the heat, despite all the water everyone was drinking. The accordions were accompanied by the high voices of women singers. The high falsetto is used to yell at their menfolk when they are in fields far across the valley.

I got quite a lot of looks as an obvious strange outsider, but everyone was friendly. A unique experience that is just the sort of thing back-roading can bring you.

Plymouth and Portsmouth

Where you are coming from may well determine whether you use Portsmouth or Plymouth for a direct sailing to Spain. For me, it often also comes down to which has the best price/time/date. Plymouth in one way is an easier run particularly for me coming from Mid-Wales as the M5 and A38 take one right to the ferry. Portsmouth can be a bit more of a challenge if one is coming from north of London. Departure time also has an impact, I'm 250-odd miles and a good 5 hours away so it is often necessary to stay somewhere closer the night before, I'm lucky in having friends within half an hour who will put me up. It is however a cost that may need to be figured in at an early planning stage. The ferry is well signposted from M27/A27 which you will be on even if coming down the A3 from London.

I can recommend camping at the Pub with No Name (aka The White Horse) at Priors Dean near Petersfield (http://www.pubwithnoname.co.uk/). It is 5 minutes from the A3 at Petersfield and a straight run to or from the ferry. For probably 50 years there has been no sign hanging in the frame. They serve most excellent beers; a good night's sleep guaranteed by the No Name Strong. The food is also well varied and delicious. The camping field is within staggering distance. There aren't any showers but there is a toilet which is open all night. £10 the night.

The food on board the ferry is good and the prices are pretty reasonable; a pint at £3.50, a main course meal in the self-service restaurant is about £7.50. If you need any special shopping do it before entering Portsmouth as the motorway funnels you to the quayside and there is not much in the way of easily accessible shops close by. Also, by the time you are getting close and the excitement is building, one just wants to be booked in and feel the adventure starting.

I remember the days when ten bikes at a time was about the norm, these days a hundred is low. When following other bikes on board be aware that you will nearly always be going down to the bottom deck down a long steel ramp. Do wait up a bit at the top and make sure the bottom is going to be clear by the time you get down there, it is not a great place to be trying to stop halfway down. Brittany Ferries' policy on the bigger ferries is to put all motorbikes on the very bottom deck where they have special ratchet sets for tying the bikes down. First bikes down are likely to be up against a wall where you will have to push your bike backward in order turn it round to get out at the other end. As there are the wire hawsers and other deck furniture associated with the tie downs it can be tricky, but I'm sure other bikers will help you if you need a hand. If you have a massive bike, unless you have a Goldwing with reverse, I'd make sure you aren't first on. If you put a bike on the centre-stand, with help you can swivel it round, sliding on the steel deck. A **word of warning** - I have had my seat scratched by rust on the 'cushion' placed on the seat under the ratchet strap, as it is tightened up the 'cushion' slides over the seat a bit, so have a rag or something handy in case. The bike always goes on the side stand as is this by far the most secure way. It's all a bit rushed when you get down there and I just have a rucksack or tail-bag that is easily removed from the bike and has just the necessities for the night. I even leave my helmet on the bike. The decks are locked during the passage. There is a lot of stairs to go up and struggling in full jacket and carrying two panniers isn't fun. Grab that one bag and get upstairs is my technique.

Although fuel maybe cheaper in Spain I tend to make sure I have a reasonably full tank going on board, then when you come off in Spain you

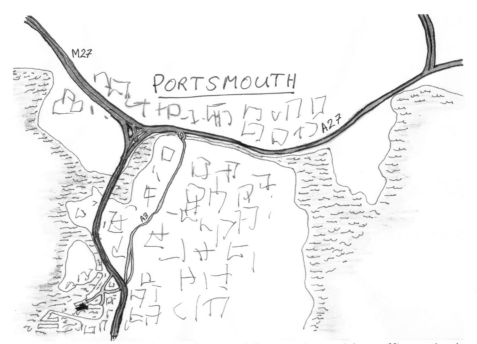

have one less thing to think about whilst coping with traffic and where you are going. For Portsmouth this generally means motorway services, at Plymouth there is a big Sainsbury's just as you come off the A38 turning into the city, good for any supplies and with a petrol station and a cafe if you are a bit early. It is a bit of a trek through the city centre so do keep an eye on which lane to get into for the various roundabouts. I have also travelled down through France. The ferry to Cherbourg is a lot cheaper. But when fuel prices are high the cost of that plus probably one night's accommodation and food on the way down can outweigh arriving in Spain rested and ready to go. The nearly a thousand kilometres largely on motorways can square one's back tyre horribly.

On some ferries you can book a reclining seat as a cheap alternative to a cabin. They don't recline a lot and one doesn't often get a decent night's kip, however finding a piece of floor to stretch out on does help, and using ear plugs!

Don't leave any alarms or parking lights active on your bike or car! Very embarrassing when it has a flat battery on arrival, having shrieked itself hoarse all crossing.

If you decide to go through France I would check for the latest on their regulations as they seem to change them regularly and come up with new bright ideas.

Going through France

When fuel prices are low and if you can spare the time, this becomes a much more attractive proposition. But it really means the expense of at least one night, and meals in France as well as the fuel to get you into Spain. Unless of course you have your own attractions, perhaps the Millau Bridge. Best view is from below apparently.

I have mostly gone Portsmouth to Cherbourg though I did try St Malo once. St Malo is a longer and more expensive crossing and the one and a half to two hours it will probably take you to get to Avranches (level with St Malo) seem to be a fair exchange. I used the smaller D-2 down the west side of the peninsular rather than the main N-13. I did the motorway Rennes to Nantes. One time I went straight down the motorways past Bourdeaux and Biarritz to Spain (after a night with a friend near Nantes). It was very boring. This is going to be a thousand kilometres and is likely to take at least twelve hours in all. Newhaven - Dieppe is also a possibility.

I had other friends near Limoges at Jumilhac-le-Grand so the other times I went via Poitiers but used some great back roads down through Confolens. By the way, Jumilhac has a fantastic castle and is on both the Camino de Santiago and the Richard the Lionheart routes. From there I took the smaller roads through Perigeux, Bergerac, Marmande and Mont-de-Marsan. I didn't stop in them but these towns may well be worth it. Mont is in the Lande, a great area of pine forests and there are quite a few campsites that could be of use. On to Orthez for the St Jean-Pied-de-Port and Roncevalles route through the Pyrenees or head for Pau/Oloron-Ste-Marie and go through to Jaca on the Spanish side. There is now the incredibly long Túnel de Somport on the N-330 from France to Spain. It can be more fun to take the old N-330A as it is now called, you need to get off the N-134 (French) about half a kilometre before the tunnel, at Les Forges d'Abel.

Do be aware that there can be snow and ice in the Pyrenees well into June and if travelling early or late in the year it can be important to check that any high passes on your route are open.

To say it again; never take the weather in Spain for granted. Terry Gilliam spent a lot of money and effort trying to make a film of Don Quixote in Spain and was totally washed out by un-seasonal weather. He has finally managed to have another go...

Really Useful Stuff

You might like to start moving your supper time to a little later a week or more before you leave; towards 8pm as the Spanish often don't eat until 8 or 9pm. As a consequence many restaurants don't really start serving till then or the proper chef won't have come in.

What to take if you are camping at least some of the time

A decent (-0°) sleeping bag because the *meseta* (central table of Spain) is at least as high as the top of Snowdon and some of my favourite campsites are above 3,500'. It can be cold at night even in June/July. I have found snow in mid-June on a high point I rode to in the Sierra de la Demanda. Take an inner bag and if it is hot you can always sleep on top of the warmer bag. I took a lightweight bag in, I think, September one year and it went down to freezing point in the night – not a lot of fun. I only take basic cooking equipment as one eats out so much and most campsites will have a bar/cafe where you can get an evening meal for a few euros. Camping gas stove and utensils are useful, a billy to heat up tinned food (I like the local recipe – *cocido* or *fabada* etc.) that you can get in many petrol station shops or in a supermarket. An old tin tea pot to brew Greek style coffee (for me a morning essential), plus an aluminium water bottle. I travel with bread, a *chorizo* sausage, some *manchego* cheese and a piece of fruit. This is often my lunch or if I ate big at lunch time, then my supper.

Do take at least one fleece unless perhaps you are skipping 'Spain' and just blasting down to that weird land of the Costas.

I take my oldest underwear and 'T' shirts, maybe 2 sets, these can be thrown away before you return to make more room for wine and chorizo. Generally clothing washed in your evening shower will dry in a day. One set of smarter trousers and short-sleeved shirt and light shoes for going on *paseo*. In other words it's easy to take too much and you can always buy a nice Spanish 'T' shirt if you need one.

Riding gear

This is a personal choice. I have Gialli denim jacket and jeans with a certain amount of protection in and see this as a compromise between ultimate leathers/goretex protection and comfort in very hot conditions. NOTE: kevlar jeans that are 'water resistant' do not wick away the sweat - boil in the bag! If the air is at 40° and you are cooking in your leather shell you will dehydrate, concentration and skill will suffer. Mind you I won't ride in a 'T' shirt and shorts, for me that is too much risk. A water bottle is important. When it is hot, drink at least a little at every stop. The air is often very dry and will suck moisture from you. On the mountain roads and in small villages you will find water taps - *fuente*, often splashing into a trough, the water will be beautiful to drink (unless it actually says *non-potable*), I refill my bottles with fresh every time.

Maps versus SatNav

I buy the Michelin 1:400 000 or better scale maps every other year (they build a lot of new roads in Spain, or upgrade and change the numbers). Depending on the areas you are going to cover, maps 573,575,576 might be sufficient. It is worth having the greater detail than a map of the whole of Spain which will miss out loads of roads and is really only any good for motorway travel. I also use a pretty good Michelin Atlas that I bought in Spain, it is wire bound and the pages unfold; scale 1:350 000, which shows most of the wonderful little back-roads as well as campsites (though I have found this information sometimes out of date). A SatNav can be good if you are going into cities but if you use it in the country you will invariably go on more major routes and not find or take by mistake the wonderful hidden routes of the land. Don't be misled by the road colours on the map; yes the red 'N' roads are like our (UK) 'A' roads but yellow roads can be nearly as good as the red ones and are not as minor as UK 'B' roads. The white ones are more like UK best 'B' roads and I use them all the time. The 'N' roads generally run along valleys and though you get to go through towns and villages the scenery often stays similar. If you go cross-country to your objective on yellow and white roads you will go through hidden valleys, pretty little villages and all sorts of different scenery. Generally road surfaces are good on all roads and particularly if you travel in the early afternoon you will find very little traffic; all the Spanish are eating and/or having a siesta. I think of the map road colouring as more indicative of traffic volume than size of carriageway.

Other equipment

I always take binoculars with me for birdwatching in Spain. I love watching the eagles and exotic birds like Bee-eaters or Rollers and there can be wonderful opportunities for dolphin and whale watching if going by ferry from the UK, particularly when crossing the abyssal drop to and from the deep part of the Bay of Biscay. I carry a small rucksack (for walking excursions in Spain) and use this on-board the ferry packed with only the things one needs during the sailing, rather than trying to lug all my gear upstairs. The vehicle decks are off-limits unless accompanied anyway and really very secure. I do take a sweater and jacket as it can be surprisingly cold out on deck.

A small camera, though these days people just seem to use their smart-phone. I believe the best way of recording your adventure is to take a journal. As you sip your evening *cerveza* and munch *tapas* in the late sun in the Plaza Mayor, make notes of those little wonders you found and experienced, draw a little map or sketch. This will embed the memory in your brain in a way a few snaps will not.

Sunscreen, do put on your face which the wind will dry, even then I find sometimes I get wind burn (of course I ride with an open face helmet, the better to smell the country).

A basic First Aid and Sewing kit. The needle can be useful for splinters. Turmeric (the cooking spice) as it is antibacterial, antiseptic, and DRY, use on any scratch, graze or picked at insect bite to stop infection and scab easily, but be aware that it stains things bright yellow, end of your nose might look a little odd.

Essential paperwork

AT TIME OF GOING TO PRESS CHANGES TO REGULATIONS AND REQUIREMENTS DUE TO THE BREXIT VOTE ARE UNKNOWN.

A Spanish (EU) legal requirement is carrying a spare light bulbs kit and a fluorescent jacket and to be on the safe side maybe carry a compact warning triangle if you can fit it in − (there are ones designed for *motos*), definitely carry one in a car. If you are going to cross into France then at least one French standard breathalyser should be carried though I have been told the police will now sell you one instead of fining you for not having it.

There is a standardised European Accident Report Form which is a two-parter that both parties fill out, this simplifies any language or disagreement problem and is worth carrying (I've never used it yet though). You can download and print these from **www. http://cartraveldocs.com/** or buy copies from various outlets.

Notes from 'ThinkSpain', 9/4/2015. http://www.thinkspain.com/

Motoring Association **AutoScout24** has reminded drivers in Spain of the documents they are required by law to carry in their car, those which are recommended but not obligatory, and possible fines for not having them if they are stopped.

The vehicle registration document – known in the UK as a VRD and in Spain as a 'circulation permit' – must be held in the glove-box, and copies are not acceptable. This document gives full details of the make and model, registration number and date of registration, technical information including chassis number, engine cubic capacity and horse power, as well as full data about the registered owner.

If it is not carried, or the ITV – Spain's answer to an MOT – is out of date, the driver will be fined up to €500 if caught.

Motorists should always have their driving licence with them – the original, not a copy – on pain of a fine starting at €10. I carry a colour photocopy as well.

Your passport - Police do stop foreign drivers to check ID.

If the licence is out of date, the fine rises to €200 and if the person has lost his or her licence due to motoring offences or health issues and is driving regardless of this, the sanction goes up to €500.

A Green Card used to be obligatory but now most insurances will have a relevant paragraph included on the schedule or policy to show you have got the minimum legal level of cover inside Europe - make sure you have it.

Carrying a copy of your insurance policy schedule and proof of premium payment is a very good idea, perhaps located separately from your wallet on the vehicle.

In the case of involvement in an accident, it is obligatory to give insurance details to the other party, or if you need to ring your insurance company in the event of a single-vehicle accident or breakdown.

Not having insurance means the vehicle will be instantly impounded and a fine ranging from €601 to €3,005 payable.

There is also a little-known rule in Spain obliging a motorist to stop at the scene of an accident and give assistance as necessary (bare minimum is to call 112, where it should be possible to obtain an English speaking operator); although there was in the past an obligation to ferry an injured person to the nearest first aid post, current best practice advises against this owing to likelihood of spinal injuries etc.

However, failure to assist a person in danger is a criminal offence, unlike in Britain where it is perfectly legal to stand and watch someone in serious trouble!

Speed trap detectors: You are **NOT allowed to have a radar speed detector** in/on your vehicle, let alone use one.

Note that the Breathalyser alcohol limit is 50mg in 100mg, with a lower figure of 30mg for drivers who have had less than two years' driving experience since passing their test. UK is 80mg.

If you are going to drink, do not drive. In some areas, particularly the touristy ones, the Guardia Civil may have roadblocks in place in the early hours and will require every driver to take a breath test. You can be jailed depending on your alcohol level. And can be also be jailed if you refuse to take the breath test, depending on how the Guardia Civil thinks about your physical state.

A GB sticker on the back of your vehicle - (BREXIT?)

Headlamp converters (stickers you put on your headlights when you're driving on the right, so your lights don't dazzle motorists coming the other way).

If you usually wear glasses or contact lenses, you must carry a spare pair with you. Make sure everyone in a car wears a seat belt at all times - driver gets fined.

Motorcyclists in Spain

Moto's are subject to the same laws as other road users, including the reflective jacket rule, which has to be worn by law if you dismount from the bike and stand on the highway. The headlight must be on dipped setting during the day, and an approved crash helmet must be worn, properly fitted and secured, at all times while riding. Penalty points can be awarded for transgressors. Otherwise, the laws are similar to other EU countries.

I carry originals of all documentation as well as photocopies of them. Theoretically, in the event of any police action the originals can be shown and the photocopies offered for their paperwork trail.

By the way, you may well find that the UK photo card Driving Licence will often act as an Identity Card as it looks very like the EU 'ID' ones (instead of pulling out your passport which I always keep in the safest possible place and not in a pickable pocket).

Don't give lip to the Guardia Civil! In any conversation a good start is the crude phrase:- *"Lo siento, mi Español es poco..."* = "I am sorry my Spanish is little." They will get the idea from this, whereas if you expressed it in perfect Spanish they would assume a higher level of understanding. They know you are trying but may understand very little. I use it in shops, anywhere, normally the result is a smile, sometimes some broken English, a friendly start to communication anyway.

In Portugal requirements are very similar but with some additions: A yellow '90' disc displayed in the car if you've held your licence for less than a year - you can apply for this from the ACP (Automovel de Club Portugal), the Portuguese motoring club.

You can pay by credit card at petrol stations but particularly in Portugal there may be a €0.50 charge for this. Consider a pre-loaded Euro Card such as the one offered by Brittany Ferries. This works like a Debit Card but it is already in Euros so you won't suddenly find extra charges or commissions appearing. I did notice a lot of self-service, unmanned petrol stations in Portugal and these are probably only going to be usable with a Card.

In Portugal the speed limit is 50 kph in built-up areas, 90 kph on open roads and 120 kph on motorways. EVEN IF THERE ARE NO SIGNS, you are supposed to know the limits, so take particular care when you enter any built-up area.

If you're caught committing a driving offence, you'll be given an on-the-spot fine, it is apparently becoming common for the police to have a Card reader for this purpose (Euro Card again).

You shouldn't use your horn at night except in cases of extreme danger.

Children under age 12 MUST NOT sit in the front.

If you're driving on motorways, don't use the green lanes - they're reserved for drivers who use the automatic payment system.

If a driver flashes their lights at you, they want you to give way.

Cars already on roundabouts have right of way.

Where there's no tram platform at the side of the road, you must give way to anyone coming off the tram and walking back to the pavement.

From **http://meravista.com/en/blogentry/driving-algarve-part-5-using-toll-roads**

A Via Verde transponder can be used to pay toll fees on any road in Portugal and Spain with electronic booths or gantries displaying the Via Verde logo. Your Via Verde transponder can also be used to pay parking fees at car parks displaying the Via Verde logo and for paying for fuel at Galp service stations offering this facility. The transponder is attached to the inside windscreen of your vehicle (or worn on an armband when riding a motorbike), and records each time you pass under an electronic toll.

Toll operators, Via Verde, have a user-friendly website, available in Portuguese, Spanish and English, where you can request a personal login to access your account and view detailed statements of your activity and charges.

If you're a visitor driving a Portuguese registered vehicle, such as a rental car, you can pay your tolls at a local Post Office, Pay Shops and most Galp motorway service stations. Simply provide your registration number and your bill will be generated. Some rental companies have fitted their vehicles with transponders, so check with the hire company when making your booking. If you're driving a vehicle with foreign number plates, you have a choice of methods for paying your tolls including hiring a transponder or pre-paying. Information on the various options available can be found in English on the Via Verde website.

If you've used the toll roads in a Portuguese registered vehicle and you don't have a transponder, you can check how much you owe by visiting the Post Office website CCT and entering your vehicle registration number.

It is always going to be worth checking on-line for the latest news particularly if you are planning a lot of driving/riding in Portugal, as things change. For instance, I have heard that at least some of the *autopista peage* (toll) roads that were built with EU money may be required to give up charging; anecdotally I have heard that small toll charges against foreign number plates are not pursued, but I wouldn't count on it.

Of course you will likely see plenty of road users apparently ignoring many of the rules, but they are locals and know when, where and what they can probably get away with. It may well not apply to *guiri - extranjeros* foreigners. A case in point being some local drivers' attitude to the fairly common radar- controlled traffic lights.

General riding/driving tips

Stick to speed limits through villages and towns. This is where nearly all speed traps/lurking Guardia Civil or Policia Local will be. Obey 'STOP' signs, you can get fined or at the least attract a 'telling off' for scooting through as if it was a give-way. Ride with your lights on.

Radar speed controls. These are common in Spain and ubiquitous in Portugal.

These are often at the entrances to villages or towns even on 'N' roads; *"ATENCIÓN – A MAS VELOCIDAD SEMAFORO CERRADO"* (I bet you can work out what it means). They have two flashing amber lights to warn you of the speed restriction. If you, **OR** the vehicle behind you is going too fast it will trigger a red stop light a little further on. As you reach it, having slowed right down it will change to flashing amber warning again, and you are free to go on. You are supposed to slow sufficiently to stop if it stays red. **Beware!** The locals will know exactly how it works and will in effect, keep

their speed and drive straight through it. Though sometimes it may be linked to a cross-light, so keep an eye on your mirror and if you have any doubts of what is happening (or in any other road event), indicate, pull over and check your map or something till you see what is going on.

In cities in particular, if you are turning onto a side road on a green light but there is an eye level flashing amber light this will indicate that you can proceed but with caution and usually means there is a pedestrian crossing with pedestrian right of way as you turn - you must give way to the feet!

Issues with 'T' junctions and roundabouts

In the early days of my journeys I used to have two diagrams in the clear, tank bag pocket where I could quickly check them. These are the two easiest potentially fatal things to get wrong. Obvious if there is immediate traffic but if deserted or you are a little tired....

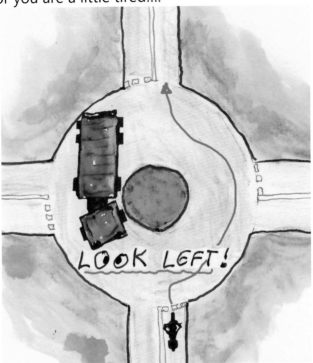

Roundabouts. Actually much improved these days as the road layout now often splits the carriageway at the roundabout and points you in the right direction, but remember which way to check and to go round. There is also the fact that in Spain the vehicle in the outside lane has right of way so most drivers don't go into the middle even if going straight on in case they can't cross to the outside... There are also an increasing number of so called turbo-roundabouts in which you are required to choose your destination lane before arrival and stick to it - hairy. Take with extreme care and watch for lorries who may not manage the inner lanes cleanly!

Give-Way T junction. This is worst when you are on a minor road that does not have a centre-line marked and when there is no other traffic or when exiting a petrol station or roadside cafe/bar. Very, very easy to look the wrong way and then pull across the road onto the wrong side. Even with more than 15 years' experience of driving in Spain I sometimes catch myself nearly doing it. NOTE;- IF THE ROAD SIGNS ON YOUR VERGE ARE SHOWING THEIR BACKS – DOH!

Turning across a main road onto a side road. Look for the sign showing you **MUST** slip off the road to your right before turning to cross the main carriageway. DO NOT TRY AND TURN FROM THE CENTRE OF THE ROAD.

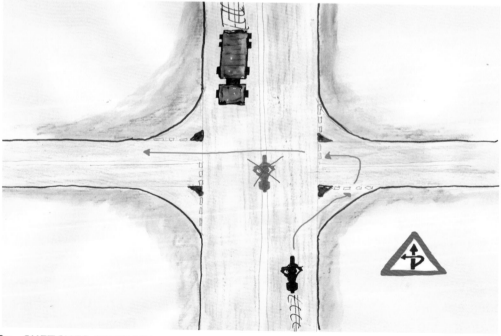

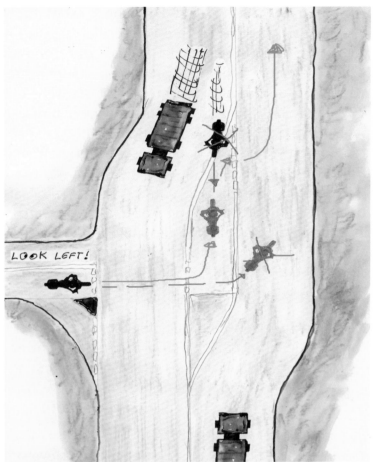

LOOK LEFT!

Joining a more major road. When joining a bigger road from a side road there will quite often be a slip road marked out in the centre of the road, you get onto this and follow it till the give-way markings and then join the main carriageway. Even if there is nothing coming, the Guardia may not like you crossing straight over and there is a good reason; there are lots of Spanish who drive their Mercedes or BMW VERY FAST and this manoeuvre gives time for a second look and increased speed before you join the main carriageway. It is also not advisable to use this extra bit of carriageway for overtaking, as a vehicle can enter that area from the side road AND STAY THERE whilst waiting to join the main carriageway.

DO KEEP AN EYE ON THAT MIRROR, YOU MAY THINK YOU ARE THE FASTEST THING ABOUT BUT... THAT MERCBEEMER DOING 130 CAN COME UP AWFULLY QUICK. Wherever possible with a following vehicle that has caught me up, I look for a place to wave them round, at least that way it happens when I want it to.

You will notice that many bends except on the back-est of roads have blue advisory speed limits posted, these are very useful because despite the fact that they are generally a very cautious guide, they do indicate quite consistently the severity of the bend. If you have been unable to see where the road goes ahead up the hillside (probably because it is only 6 mts almost directly above you), then a 30 sign means one of those bottom gear hairpins, possibly with dodgy camber and also possibly with grit, thrown by vehicles cutting onto the hard shoulder. This is a feature of many Spanish roads, a bit of extra carriageway width for the trucks without the cost of tarmac. It does mean a bike can stop on the verge pretty safely in a lot of places, for a photo opportunity or whatever. BUT do watch out for the dreaded foot-slide-away that has you dropping the bike, or crawling out from underneath. Don't worry, pride is generally hurt more than you or the bike and you've still got the view - I've had it happen enough times...

Group riding tips

There is quite an art to leading a group of riders. You can of course just agree the final destination, but in a way this detracts from the group experience and people can get lost or miss out on something great that has been spotted. It may be good to rotate the leader position so that everyone gets a chance to relax a bit, not worrying about the route.

The keenest/quickest rider will likely be right behind you. Don't let them 'push' you faster than suits. If possible don't have the slowest last; harder to keep them in sight.

The group will be travelling at the speed of the slowest so keep the 'keenite' happy, do some sections where there is a rendezvous point ahead that everybody can find and they can go at their own speed to get there.

Who has the lowest tank mileage? – Set the stops.

Print a 'business' card with the group's mobile phone numbers on and a reminder that the:-

EMERGENCY SERVICES ARE ON: 112

In discussion find a daily rhythm that suits; perhaps, leave by 9 am at latest, lunch at 1-2 plus 'siesta' half hour relaxation, *tapa* stop 4, supper 8-9?

If you are parking your *moto* on a pavement (not the problem it is in the UK) to go and look at a site or stroll around, try asking the nearest bar if it is okay to leave the bikes there whilst you take a little walk. They'll tell you if there is a problem or local ordinance restricting parking, and may well offer to watch them for you.

Watch out for hotels charging extra for breakfast (not always included, not always great), you may get better in the corner bar depending on where you are – check it out the night before.

Generally mobile signal is better than in Wales, but there are places in the high back of beyond where signal is poor or intermittent. It might be worth warning those back home when you are going to these areas that you may not be in touch for a night or so. An example is the wonderful Camping Valle Enmedio near Peguerinos in the Sierra de Guadarrama at an altitude of 1500 mts (just short of 5,000').

You might like to get nitrogen in your tyres before you go. The larger molecule = less leakage through tyre walls etc. And does not change pressure with heat or altitude. Many 'ATS' do this for a minimal fee.

A little point: when you get a drink or some *tapas* in a bar or restaurant, unless they ask you to pay straight away, don't ask for the bill - *la cuenta por favor*, or how much - *¿quanto es?* Immediately. The custom is to pay at the end, after you have enjoyed the refreshment; paying before is considered a bit rude - as if you know you won't want anything else. In my experience it is very rare for there to be any attempt to limit how long you stay after you have finished even one coffee. It is part of the different attitude to life, open yourself up to it, embrace it. Good service and good refreshment though does deserve a tip (10% perhaps), in my opinion.

IMPORTANT NOTE FOR THE ENGLISH! To get something like an English cup of tea you need to be quite specific. *"Té negro con leche fría aparte, por favor."* - Tea (black), with milk (cold) apart, or on the side, please. If asked about the *agua* it is *caliente* you want. Theoretically, you should ask for an *infusión de té* but in some places they'll give you a chilled tea. The tea needs to be black or you'll get rooibos/red tea, camomile or something with a lot of flowers in it (you may get it black with flowers anyway as they don't always have plain tea bags). If you just ask for *"Té negro con leche,"* you'll get the nearest tea bag in frothy hot milk from the expresso machine - this will be vile! Even getting the request right does not guarantee an 'English cup of tea', it doesn't bother me because I only drink *café solo* or a herb tea - *infusión de manzanilla*, camomile tea or *té menta,* mint tea. But my wife needed her sense of humour at times.

Spanish people in all but perhaps the big cities greet each other a lot. Social interaction is the norm. They may well spot you as *extranjero* and not expect anything. But a polite *hola* or *buenas dias* will always get a response. Whenever someone meets your eye, acknowledge and say what you can... You will find that the *buenas dias* may drift far into abbreviation depending where you are: *buena - buendia - buenas*. The same happens with the goodbye; *hasta luego*, it can be cut down to almost *logo*. They are also quite tactile and will touch your arm or pat your shoulder in conversation, give kids (not their own) a cheek squeeze or other sign of approbation, and quite quickly upon getting to know you expect the double cheek kiss. Go with it, all part of being part of a different culture. I remember being quite surprised when my Madrid friend patted a child that was playing around the tables where we were having coffee. Outside the big city and tourist areas people look out for each other. Of course there can be, for young women in particular at clubs or bars, the odd man who will try and take advantage of this - a firm *bastante* - enough! Should be sufficient.

Hablar Español - speak Spanish. Bad Spanish works!

A 'club' or 'disco' or 'dancing' 'hotel' right on the outskirts of a town or a field or two away from it with a big weedy car park is more than likely a brothel.

City visits

Consider leaving your vehicle in a smaller town and catching an express coach or train into the big city. I have done this to visit Madrid for a night leaving my *moto* in the hostal car park in Burgos. Riding or driving into Madrid is not a lot of fun (in my experience).

Roads on a Michelin map with broken lines on one side are un-surfaced and maybe rough.

Camping

Campsites in Spain are variable and this is mainly due to the different functions that they predominately cater for. There are ones that are largely used for weekend partying by younger people (El Escorial), and ones which are predominately static caravans lived in most of the year or at least every weekend, as a retreat from the big city (a number around Madrid which are unlikely to take in any travellers). There are also ones on many tourist routes that have a large turnover of foreigners on their way to and from the south. And small local municipal sites catering for families with local connections in the main, but who will take in travellers. As well as largely Spanish campsites that are not necessarily advertised at all. And sites that combine many of these uses.

One year I left Granada at 2pm (46°) after visiting the Alhambra. I rode until I was north of Madrid, around 500 km, it took me three campsites before I found one that would take me. The others all being weekend escapes from Madrid filled with static pitches.

It is common for the nightly cost to be made up of a number of items; vehicle, tent or caravan (perhaps by size) and number of persons.

One night, one *moto*, one adult and a small tent in 2016 was €10 - €15 in the places I visited.

Most sites will be well equipped with showers, toilets and have a shop and bar or restaurant and most now have free Wifi ('*wee-fee*' if you are asking about it). Sit in your tent and log in! Oops, showing my lack of 'Smart-Phone' - thing.

On my travels in Spain I generally combine the odd night in a hostal or parador (€40-€80) and camping at (€10-€15), to even it up.

Unless you are staying close to sea level or going straight to Andalucia I do advise being prepared for night time temperatures to drop outside of high summer. Not that many campsites will have grassed plots and the ground will be HARD; a small blow-up mattress I have found well worth the carrying. As said earlier, if it's warm you have the additional comfort of sleeping on top of your winter-weight sleeping bag. Ear plugs can certainly be handy in the busier campsites. When I say 'free' camping I mean it's not a defined pitch, you can choose where to set up within the area.

Camping Playa Arenillas - Islares

This is the nicest campsite I have found close to Bilbao and Santander. There are loads of others though, so I may have missed better. It has lots of amenities including drying machines, in case you have been sampling the source of the Costa Verde. I am guessing in high season it may get a pretty packed as it is popular with families because of the lovely beach. In high season it may be worth contacting them directly through their website (as addresses change from time to time, it is best to search for it on the internet), to make sure they will have space for you.

Camping Rio Nela - Trespaderne

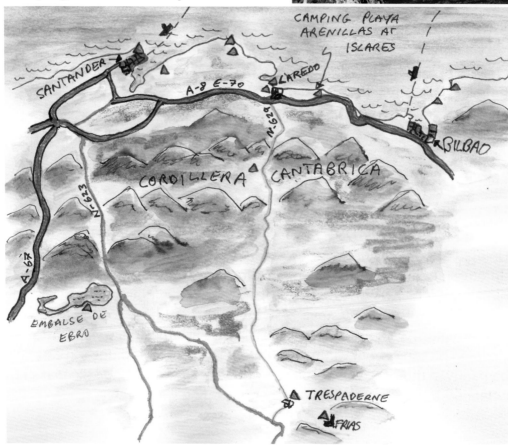

This a typical Spanish family site but does take passers-by. I was given a nice spot between two cabins close to the shower block. Admittedly this was out of high season. It suited me for the run to the ferry in the morning and a last evening that was very Spanish. 2016 rates - *Moto* €3.50, *adulto* 5.50, family tent €4.50, maybe a small one would be less.

Camping Fuentes Blancas - Burgos

A typical city site really, has all the normal facilities. It is generally pleasant

enough but there is not a late return bus from town to the site (it is 3 km) so if you want an evening enjoying the city a taxi is the way, not expensive if shared. I have to say because this is my favourite city in Spain and the evening *paseo* is so good I nearly always make this one of my hostal nights either staying in Hostal Acuarela close to the Plaza de España where you are minutes walk from the Plaza Mayor or a little cheaper at the Hostal Acanto where there is the short, cheap bus ride into town.

Camping D'Oremor - near Madrid

This is a family site for *madrileños* but they did find space for me and my little tent. A nice lot of trees on the site. It was early June 2010 and I had left Granada at 2pm where it was over 45°, about 500 km later and 50 km north of Madrid I needed to stop for the night. I tried two other campsites marked on the map closer to Madrid, but they wouldn't take even me and my one-man tent. Obviously residential/weekend sites. If you do need to spend a night anywhere near to Madrid, a bit of research would be a good idea.

It is close to Cabanillas de la Sierra 50 km exit of the N-1/E-5.

Camping Valle Enmedio - Peguerinos, El Escorial

This is a favourite place to stay. (see P113) It is in a high valley of the Sierra de Guadarrama (1500 mts - 5,000'). Cool when it's baking a few miles away in El Escorial, spectacular scenery and lots of pine trees. Restaurant/bar and all the normal amenities with loads of good walking routes in the mountains.

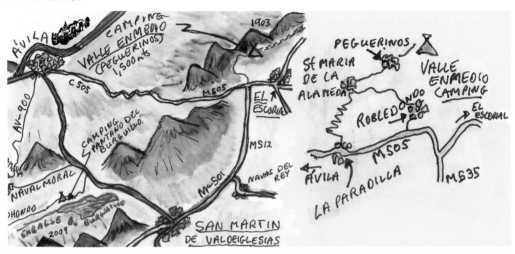

My friend Rosario who works there explained their opening times; We will be open in June from 1st to the 17th, just the weekends, and from the 17th to the 11th of September every day. They have some great pictures of all the cabins covered in snow! Wifi and mobiles - not really! If I didn't have so many other places to get to, I think it would be wonderful to stay a week in both this and Casavieja, birdwatching and walking the area. There are a lot of cheeky Nuthatches and it is lovely to watch the Crested Tits feeding between the pine needles. And perhaps catch glimpses of eagles

overhead. One could also use this as a base to visit El Escorial, Segovia, Avíla or even Madrid, perhaps finding a safe place to leave your vehicle in El Escorial and taking public transport into the city.

Camping Casavieja (Gredos)

Another high mountain campsite which is very pleasant. They have some enormous red squirrels, twice the size of ours, who drop half-eaten pine cones on you from the tops of the pine trees. As with Enmedio, it is lovely sitting by your tent in the evening with a beer, listening to the sigh of a breeze through the needles, glimpsing a soaring eagle and smelling

the fragrance of the pines.

With all these campsites, I have always just turned up on the day but this has rarely been during the high - August season so they may not be quite so idyllic when very busy.

Camping Sierra de Gata - Plascencia

No 'free' camping space, so I was on a pitch and I guess in the high season they may be short of room. A nice situation with the river and amenities.

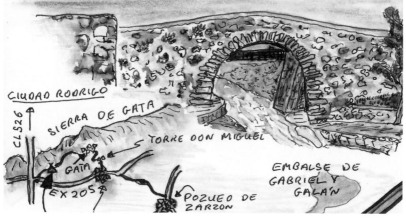

Camping Arlanza - Quintanar de la Sierra (Burgos)

I do love staying here. There is a 'free' camping space, a lot of it across a wooden bridge over the river that runs through the site. Hah-hah, you can ride your *moto* over there but no four wheelers can join you. The *weefee* seems to reach all over and the facilities are good, the staff of the site and of the restaurant/bar very helpful and obliging, even pretty much out of season. A good base for exploring the wonderful Sierra de la Demanda.

"TARIFAS 2016:   *A estos precios se les añadirá el IVA en vigor. Tempora Alta: Semana Santa, Julio y Agosto.

Temporada Baja: resto de los meses que el Camping permanezca abierto.

ACAMPADA Y PARCELAS*

PARCELA incluye: Caravana, vehículo y toma de electricidad 6A 9,75 €/DIA

ADULTO	3,60 €/DIA
NIÑO	2,80 €/DIA
TIENDA INDIVIDUAL	3,00 €/DIA
TIENDA COLECTIVA	4,00 €/DIA
COCHE	3,50 €/DIA
AUTOCARAVANA	7,00 €/DIA
CARAVANA	4,00 €/DIA
MOTOCICLETA	2,75 €/DIA
AUTOBÚS	8,00 €/DIA
PERRO	1,50 €/DIA"

Camping Cañón del Rio Lobos - Ucero

I have not stayed in it, but it looks good. In the bottom of the *cañón* and close to the river. Down here it feels like a separate little world. The river has some BIG fish in it. I've seen them from the *mirador* at the top of cliffs!

'Wild' Camping

Spain is a big country with lots of empty space and natural areas and it can be tempting to just stick up a tent, up some track that seems to go no-where. But, forest fires are a very dangerous potential hazard and the locals are going to be wary. The chances are someone has seen you and may report you. I have often been surprised by coming upon elderly people walking up some minor road apparently absolutely miles from anywhere. No wonder they live longer than us. 'Wild' camping is possible but I would always suggest finding somewhere that you can ask for, and gain permission to do so. Be aware that due to the very real danger of fires in this dry country, police and wardens are very much on the watch for illegal camping and will come down on you especially hard if you light a fire. In very dry times even where there are barbecues built at picnic spots these may be banned from being used by local ordinances.

The only place I have camped 'wild' was on the beach north of Carboneras near Almeria. There were many tracks leading down to the sandy beach and I could see others setting up for the night.

__Simple Spanish__

Note in Spanish vowels don't change their sound depending on who is standing next to them. It is worth getting at least a small phrase book, one that gives you an idea how to pronounce each word.

Yes - *sí*
No - *no*
Never - *nunca*
Please - *por favor*
Thank you - *gracias*
I'm sorry - *lo siento*
Hello - *hola*
Good morning/afternoon/night - *¡Buenos días/tardes/noches!*
Goodbye - *adiós,* see you later - *hasta luego,* see you soon - *hasta pronto*
How are you? - *cómo estás*

I/me/my - *yo/me/mi* (somewhat interchangeable according to usage)
You - *usted* formal, informal *tú* or *su* (somebody you know well)
For me - *para mi*

Do you have? - *tienes*
To eat - *comer*
To sleep - *dormir*
Can I? - *puedo*
Where is - *dónde está*

Left - *izquierda*
Right - *derecho*
Straight on - *recto*
Here - *aquí*
There - *allí*
Exit - *salida*
Enter - *entrada*
Open - *abierto*
Closed - *cerrado*

I like- *me gusta*
I don't like - *no me gusta*

Toilets - *servicios,* gents - *caballeros,* ladies - *señoras,* restroom - *aseos*

More - *más*
Less - *menos*
Small - *pequeña,* little bit - *poco*
Large - *grande*
Too expensive - *muy caro,* very - *muy,* much - *mucho*

Also - *tambien*
Another - *otro,* again - *otro vez*
And - *y*
With - *con*

Water - *agua*
A glass of red/white wine - *una copa de vino tinto/blanco*
A small glass of beer in a bar - *una caña*
Bread - *pan*
Cheese - *queso*
Something - *algo*
Perhaps - *quizás*
But - *pero,* dog - *perro*

It is possible? - *¿es posible?*
Necessary - *necesario*
I need - *necesito*

Now - *ahora*
Yesterday - *ayer*
Today - *hoy*
Tomorrow - *mañana,* also morning

Come on/let's go- *venga/ ¡Vamonos!/vamos.* This and other words come from the irregular verb for to go - *ir,* it's a nightmare...
Journey - *viaje*

You will notice that there an enormous number of words in Spanish that are very similar to English or to put it another way, there are many English words that can be turned into Spanish ones with small additions and a slightly different pronunciation. You can have a lot of fun with this. But I suggest a handy dictionary if it starts going pear-shaped.

It is a favourite game with my Spanish friends; comparing and explaining colloquialisms and sayings in English, and back in Spanish that don't mean what they seem to say.

Reading List

Just books on my shelf...

The Factory of Light by Michael Jacobs. ISBN 0-7195-6173-6

Spanish Steps by Tim Moore. ISBN 0-224-06265-4

Don Quixote by Miguel Cervantes. ISBN 0-436-20515-7

Jupiter's Travels by Ted Simon. ISBN 0 14 00.5410 3

The Outlaw Josey Wales (formerly 'Gone to Texas') by Forrest Carter. ISBN 0 8600 7331 9

On Bullfighting by A.L.Kennedy ISBN 0-224-06099-6 Yellow Jersey Press (Randomhouse)

Duende by Jason Webster. ISBN 0-385-60361-4 and any of his others.

Gerald Brennan books, all good reads:

South from Granada. ISBN 0-14-016700-5

The Spanish Labyrinth. ISBN 0-521-39827-4

Roads to Santiago by Cees Nooteboom. ISBN 1-86046-419-X

Ghosts of Spain by Giles Tremlett. ISBN 0-571-22167-X

A Stranger in Spain by H.V. Morton. My copy is pre ISBN

The Shadow of the Wind by Carlos Ruiz Zafón.

Cathedral of the Sea by Ildefonso Falcones. ISBN 978-0-385-61185-5

The Basque History of the World by Mark Kurlansky. ISBN 0-099-28413-8

The Forging of a Rebel by Arturo Barea.

Winter in Madrid by C.J.Sansom. ISBN 1-4050-0546-7

The Spanish Ulcer by David Gates (history of the Peninsular war). ISBN 0-7126-9730-6

Cassell's - Colloquial Spanish. ISBN 0-304-07943-x

Birds of Europe by Lars Jonsson. ISBN 0-7136-4422-2

Back Roads of Spain by Duncan Gough. ISBN 978-0-9957454-0-7 also available as an e-book (minus some images) ASIN: B00ARY1LES.

Spanish food

The Spanish love their food with immense dedication. They are very proud of their local and provincial specialities. Part of the reason for this is that local produce is almost invariably used (of course this may not be the case in major cities and tourist areas). They also eat out incredibly frequently, and as a very fruitful consequence, bad restaurants or bars don't last long (except perhaps where there is a mainly passing trade of tourists). Some dishes come with vegetables or a salad, but quite often these will be a separate dish in their own right (not a sort of garnish slung on the side). There is only space to mention a few of my favourites: *Sopa castellana* - Castilian soup, a meal in itself with lots of garlic, serrano ham and paprika often red pepper and maybe chicken stock with generally an egg dropped into the top (either poached by the soup or put in the oven for a short while); *Pulpo Gallego* - Galician octopus, a very simple dish of generally cold sliced octopus on warm, boiled potatoes with a dusting of paprika on the top; *Berenjenas con miel* - fried aubergine slices drizzled with honey, and *Bocadillos* - a small Spanish loaf of bread with an enormous number of possible fillings, I particularly like one with fresh *tortilla* in it. Remember a *tortilla* in Spain is a juicy, thick omelette with potatoes and onion in it, not a flat Mexican pancake. Many meat dishes are *asado* - roasted, sometimes in a huge wood-fired oven a bit like a pizza oven. For instance, *cordero asado* - roast lamb. Go into the Restaurante Casa Ojeda on the Plaza de la Libertad, Burgos, and you will see one in action. Be aware that not much of an animal is ever wasted and though you might know that *cerdo* is pork, if you don't know what part is on the menu it could be anything from the cheeks to the trotters (boiled probably in the latter case). It can always be worth asking about vegetables, the simplest way is to just say *¿con vegetales/ verduras?* in a questioning voice. It may take you a little while to sort out the reply, but you might catch the following; *patatas* - potatoes, *cebolla* - onion, *col* - cabbage, *judías verdes* - green beans, *ensilada* - salad. *Morcilla* is a blood sausage, particularly good in Burgos. *Callos* is an intestine tapa mentioned earlier.

Recipes to get you going. Please note these are not necessarily the proper traditional way to do it, but it works for me. You can work out the quantities depending on how many you are catering for.

I enjoy doing a *tapas* evening for friends. I use small earthenware dishes, a little good olive oil and chopped garlic in the bottom, then in separate dishes; about 10mm thick slices of *chorizo*; decent sized prawns; some tinned octopus or calamares, then add a sprinkle of paprika on the top. Most of these only need to go in the oven long enough to heat through and be sizzling. Paprika or *pimentón* comes in different grades from *dulce* - sweet, *agridulce* - bittersweet/mild and *picante* - hot, they can also be 'smoked'. I prefer the smoked ones, but choose the one you like. I put oil, garlic and *vino tinto* in a lidded oven dish filled to the very brim with sliced mushrooms. I might make a *tortilla* earlier in the day as it is fine served cold or warm. If I feel keen I might grill some courgettes and roast some peppers to be drizzled with olive oil when served. A good salad, crusty bread and plenty of *vino*, what more but good company do you need?

Tortilla: I chop up a potato into 15mm squares and give them a quick blast in the microwave or a quick boil so that they are pretty much cooked. Fry chopped onion and garlic in a pan adding the potato when the onion is soft and perhaps slightly browned. A number of eggs go in a jug with some fresh thyme and get whipped up a bit. I heat olive oil till it's smoking in another frying pan, then throw the onions and potato in and pour over the eggs. Turn the heat down a little, keep an eye on the underneath of the tortilla so it doesn't stick and once lightly browned put the pan under the grill to cook the top. The inside should not be over-cooked and get dried up. I use two pans because all though traditionally you do it all in one I find

it is far more likely to stick - my pans or my technique?

Albondigas: The basis (the sauce) of this recipe comes from the excellent Australian Women's Weekly Home Library 'Easy Spanish style cookery'. I cheat with the meatballs; I get the best quality local beefburgers I can, quarter them and roll the quarters into meatballs. Brown them in a big pan and put to one side. Separately, fry finely chopped onion and garlic with some paprika in the bottom of a saucepan. Once the onion is soft, chuck in one or two cans of chopped tomatoes, a beef stock-pot dissolved in a small amount of hot water, even a squirt of tomato paste and at least one <u>cinnamon stick</u>. Simmer for at least 10 mins to get it thickening (depends on the quality of the tins how much water there is in it). Now add the meatballs and chopped, pitted green olives and simmer for another 10 mins or so to make sure the meatballs are cooked through. Take out the cinnamon sticks, if you want, scatter chopped fresh parsley on the top and serve with basmati rice (rinsed well before cooking) and cooked with turmeric in the water - flavour and colour!

The round lidded pot in the photo above, I bought in Burgos, in a hardware store just round the corner from the Hostal Acanto on the Calle Vitoria. I have bought a number of these earthenware dishes from there and love using them. You have to soak them in water for 24 hours before first use and not heat them with nothing liquid in them. But you can fry in the bottom of them, browning onions and meat etc. Add your stock and other vegetables, put the lid on and straight in the oven. And they look great when you are serving up.

Cocidos and *fabadas* are stews (for instance *fabada asturiana* from Asturias and *cocido madrileño* from Madrid). When camping I often buy these in tins from petrol stations as a simple evening meal with bread.

At home I like to make my own version particularly using the rounded pot because it is excellent for even, slow cooking. I put a good slosh of olive oil in the bottom with garlic and *dulce* paprika then throw chopped meat, vegetables (whatever is hanging about - potato, onion, courgette, aubergine - all cubed), herbs, stock and often *alubias* of some kind; butter or haricot beans - *judiones granja*. If I've got time I will roll the meat in flour seasoned with fresh thyme and paprika and brown it in a frying pan first. I always have a jar of Lidl's Freshona roasted red peppers on hand to add diced, I also pour in some of the juice from the jar. Sometimes a tin of chopped tomatoes or a splash of wine; it needs a bit of liquid but not too much because depending on the vegetables they can give up quite a lot. Pre-heat the oven to 150°C (300°F, Gas mark 2) as you are throwing things in the pot. Give an hour at that and then 2-3 hours at 100°C (220°F, Gas mark 1/4).

The beakers are actually yoghurt pots collected over the years from Brittany Ferries, unfortunately they are now using glass ones.

Griffon vulture

Golden eagle. Up to 7 1/2' wing span.

Short-toed eagle. Pale underside with barring. Quite big, up to 6' wing span. Eats snakes!

Kestrel

Booted eagle. Size of a buzzard but has light patches at ends of wings and when soaring the end 'hand' feathers are not spread

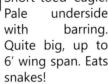

Egyptian vulture

Black kites. Only slight 'V' in tail, red kite has much deeper.

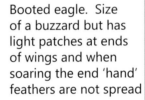

White Storks

Young azure-winged magpie

Water Pippit

Crested tit

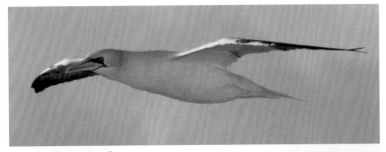

Gannet from the ferry

Gredos Ibex

Corzo - Roe deer

Red-collared Burnet Moth

Cicada

Ocellated Lizard 600mm (1') long but they can get much bigger, up to metre.

Red Admiral

Comma

Fritillary. I think the Queen of
Spain Fritillary

Swallowtail

Peacock

I'm not good at flower identification and don't know what these all are, but the variety and beauty one can find in the countryside is astounding. I think bottom left is some kind of bee orchid, the top picture is a natural Monet that my father would have loved to paint in his own special way..

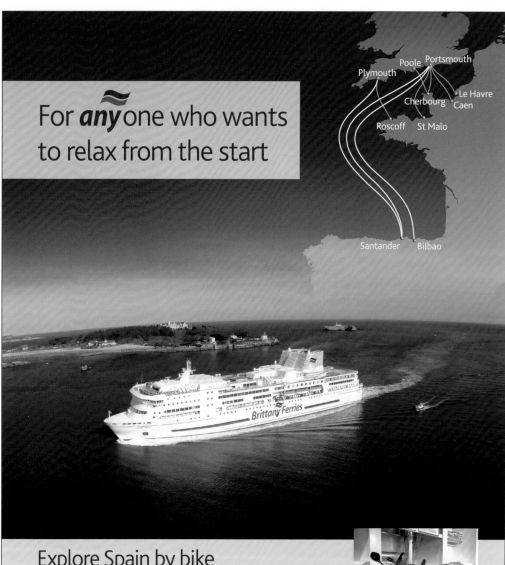

Hotels in Burgos, Spain

acuarela hostal

techroom®

www.hostalacuarela.com

reservas@hostalacuarela.com

Guardia Civil 7
09004 Burgos
Tel. (0034) 947 20 50 50

HOSTAL acanto

HOSTAL ACANTO
C/Esteban Sáez Alvarado,
3 bajo esq. C/Vitoria 261
09007 Burgos
www.hostalacanto.com
Tel. (0034) 947 482 551

I am available for basic travel suggestions (for free). Itineraries at a reasonable cost, based on the complexity and length, and occasionally personally designed and conducted tours. Just get in contact through my website. I will also be happy to receive your thoughts about the book.

Duncan Gough.

Website and contact:-

www.duncan-spanish-travel.com

Blog:-

www.duncangough.wordpress.com/

With many thanks to all the people who have helped me with comments, suggestions and criticisms.

Ruth Shirtcliff for encouragement and editing and Jane MacNamee for the copyedit/proofing.

My wife for telling me to; "get it done!"

Been using this book to plan a trip, it's a great book, I love the hand drawn maps, very much like the Wainwright guides of the English Lakes, the book is a fountain of knowledge for anybody looking to travel in Spain.

Stuártvár Ingi Gráhámson

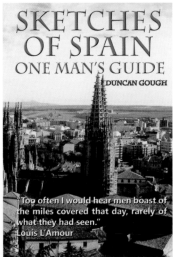
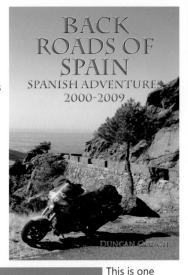
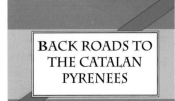
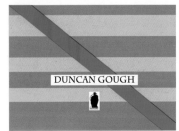
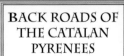

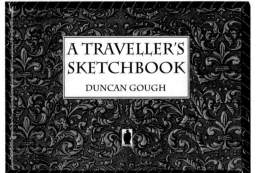